The Seven Last Words

MICHAEL H. CROSBY, OFMCap

ORBIS BOOKS

Maryknoll, New York 10545

The Catholic Foreign Mission Society of America (Maryknoll) recruits and trains people for overseas missionary service. Through Orbis Books, Maryknoll aims to foster the international dialogue that is essential to mission. The books published, however, reflect the opinions of their authors and are not meant to represent the official position of the society.

Copyright © 1994 by Michael H. Crosby, OFMCap
Published by Orbis Books, Maryknoll, NY 10545

Orbis Books gratefully acknowledges use of the following illustrations:

"Pieta" sketch by Paul Conrad. Reprinted by permission, Los Angeles Times Syndicate. "Lime Pit 1990" by Hans Burkhardt. Reprinted by permission, Jack Rutberg Fine Arts, Inc., Los Angeles, CA. Photograph by Carl de Keyzer that originally appeared on the cover of his work *God, Inc.* © Carl de Keyzer/Magnum Photos. Reprinted by permission, Magnum Photos, New York, NY. Drawing by R. S. Johnson, "Remember me, Lord, when you come into your Kingdom," used by permission of the artist. Drawing by Celso Bordignon, OFMCap, "Christ in the Fabella," used by permission of the artist. The author also wishes to thank the Dutch High Commissioner for the World's Fair Pavilion at Montreal, 1988, for use of the photo taken from the display on Religion and Culture in the Netherlands; Rev. Anton Jenkins for permission to use his meditation, "It's Not Finished"; and Jeff Fenholt for permission to share his story. For more information about Jeff Fenholt, see audiotape "Testimony" (Upland, CA: Messiah Records).

Library of Congress Cataloging-in-Publication Data

Crosby, Michael, 1940–
    The seven last words / Michael H. Crosby.
       p. cm.
    Includes bibliographical references
    ISBN 0-88344-938-2
    1. Jesus Christ—Seven last words—Meditations.   I. Title.
BT456.C76   1994
232.96'35—dc20   93-33911
                                                           CIP

Contents

Preface

Prefaces of books usually are written last. My experience with this book is the same. In this day of lap-top computers and fax machines, Robert Ellsberg of Orbis Books faxed me a sample of the page proofs for this book while I visited Bangkok. Because it is impossible to proceed with page proofs without pagination for the preface, I needed to write this book's preface in Bangkok.

The Seven Last Words represents my attempt to relate Jesus' final words from the cross to our cultural realities. Given the view of some of those realities I've witnessed in the last six hours, I think it is particularly appropriate that I write my concluding thoughts from Bangkok. In this unique culture—both non-Christian and increasingly oriented to conspicuous consumption—I have encountered face-to-face both the relevancy and irrelevancy of the cross.

It is 5:30 A.M. I am writing in my hotel room in Pattaya, so-called Sex Capital of the World. I haven't slept. The images from my last few hours are still too vivid.

Brother Raymond F. Taylor, a canonical monk who is director of Mercy Center, led me on a kind of "urban plunge" of Pattaya. Ray came here to work with refugees; he found himself ministering instead to young men from the provinces who came south in hopes of helping their families find a better way of life. They found themselves, instead, reinforcing the fetishes and lifestyles of the "rich and famous."

Before touring the bar scene, we visited the Redemptorist Center, a large retreat-type facility. Having had a few not-so-positive experiences of Catholicism's inculturation into the Thai culture, the visit offered a breath of fresh air. The murals surrounding the chapel used Thai images and settings to tell the story of Jesus (not unlike the murals at the Great Temple in Bangkok). The highlight, as in so many stories of Jesus, was the cross.

But then, touring the night spots with Raymond, I discovered that the cross not only covered the chapel walls at the Redemptorist Center, but it dangled from the ears of the prostitutes yelling for us to join them at the open-air bars and it hung around the necks of young men dancing in G-strings for those who came to buy their services. As I walked through the booths where men seek sex with boys as young as 7 or 8, I wondered how many of these children have been frequented by the clergy of all cloths, men who regularly sign themselves with that cross. For the men and women, girls and boys wearing the cross on their bodies in Pattaya it was, like the sex itself, just part of the culture, a "culture of death." That is the phrase Pope John Paul II used to describe the capitalist system, which has no qualms about coopting even the cross, provided money can be made from doing so.

The cross—relevant in the Redemptorist Center, irrelevant in the streets of Pattaya. Or is the cross ever irrelevant? Do Jesus' last words speak to all cultures, even our own "culture of death"? I believe that they do.

As I sum up this book about the words from the cross and their cultural impact, I'd like to thank Robert Ellsberg for gently but persistently hounding me to write these reflections that have been stewing in me for a decade. My editors Ginny Schauble, Joan Laflamme and Catherine Costello have again proved to be invaluable in their final rendition.

Mercy Center, Burlingame, California, provided me the forum to share my ideas for this book with a group of retreatants during the Holy Week Triduum 1993. I thank both the Center and the wonderful group members for their help in producing the final product. Finally, I would like to thank the friars involved in the life and ministry of St. Benedict's in Milwaukee, who have been my inspiration and community for the last two years. In thanks for their fraternity, I dedicate this book.

MICHAEL H. CROSBY,
OFMCap.
Bangkok, Thailand
21 August 1993

Introduction

In our novitiate, the only time we were allowed out was to see William Wyler's production of General Lew Wallace's Ben Hur. Besides the haunting, lyrical melody at the birth scene, and the awesome cracks of lightning at Jesus' death, what impressed me most were the powerful images behind those scenes of birth and crucifixion: the life and death of each of us.

I sat near the novice master. He frightened me. In the name of Jesus and Holy Obedience, he made his authority felt—tangibly and palpably—filling a room.

He intimidated us novices with his power. Yet he confused us by shrouding it with legitimacy in the name of God and Holy Obedience:

> Ours is not to wonder why.
> [In the name of the Crucified One]
> Ours is but to do and die.

So we didn't ask why until years later. And then we came to realize that the control he exercised over us in God's name through fear and intimidation was abuse. In many ways it was like a minor crucifixion for many of us.

But there in the theater, as the movie's crucifixion scene melted to resurrection, and as the sound track's music summoned the mystical drama, I heard another sound come from the novice master's seat. He was crying.

The first Calvary was set into motion by the clerical caste in order to preserve the clerical system. The justification it offered to rationalize killing the one who asked questions was "the good of the people."

"It is proper," they decreed, "that one man should die for the people."

Among those thirty-one novices — innocents experiencing our own form of violence — the cleric we called master, who did what he did for "the good of the Order," cried.

Were his tears true, or merely sentimental, or was he thinking in that darkened movie theater of the violence we were suffering at his hands? We will never know.

Besides the tears of our novice master, I also recall the movie's rendition of that Calvary scene. It was different from what I expected. I had thought I'd be hearing those seven last words from the Crucified One that have echoed through the ages. But instead, Jesus said nothing at all from the cross.

What? Nothing? This is not the way it took place according to the gospels, I thought to myself. But that was before I had studied the gospels.

The gospels as we know them today were the works of those we have come to know as Matthew, Mark, Luke, and John. So which gospel is right about those words from the cross?

Mark and Matthew say that Jesus cried out in Hebrew,

> My God, my God, why have you forsaken me?
> (Mk 15:34; Matt 27:46).

Luke renders Christ's words in a triad:

> Father forgive them, for they do not know what
> they are doing (Lk 23:34).

> Truly, I tell you, today you will be with me in
> Paradise (Lk 23:43).

> Father, into your hands I commend my spirit
> (Lk 23:46).

If we read John's account literally, it seems he was the only eyewitness to these scenes (Jn 21:20,24). He recounts that Jesus said to his mother,

> Woman, here is your son

and to the disciple whom he loved,

> Here is your mother (Jn 19:26, 27).

John also reports Jesus saying,

> I am thirsty (Jn 19:28)

and, finally, his words

> It is finished (Jn 19:30).

For centuries scholars, semanticists, and storytellers have tried to determine which words were really spoken from the cross and when.

Well over a hundred years after that gruesome Golgotha, around 150 C.E., Tatian was the first to "harmonize" the disparate sounds from the cross in his *Dietessaron*. Since then there has been anything but harmony among those who have tried to determine which words of Jesus, according to Matthew, Mark, Luke, and John, came first, second, and on until the seventh.

When I was growing up, Bishop Fulton J. Sheen was the most renowned preacher on television. His weekly show had a huge audience. But every First Friday at St. Agnes Church in Manhattan he would preach on the "Seven Last Words of Jesus." When I entered the novitiate, the first "harmonization" of those words from the cross that I read came from Bishop Sheen as well. I was inspired and haunted by his best-selling *Life of Christ*.

Around the same time Jim Bishop published his hour-by-hour account *The Day Christ Died*. He said it happened this way: First, Jesus said, "Father, forgive them," and then, "This day, you will be with me in paradise." Then he spoke to his mother and the Beloved Disciple, who was to take her home. Following this came his words of desolation, of being forsaken and thirsty; and then, finally, "Father, into your hands I commit my spirit" and "It is finished." Francis Cardinal Spellman gave his assurance, his *imprimatur*, that there was nothing in Bishop's account that was against faith and morals. It could be believed, safely, by true believers.

But *now* some scholars say that storytellers like Bishop Sheen and Jim Bishop—and Matthew, Mark, Luke, and John—were wrong, that we can't be sure if any of those words came from Jesus. These scholars have concluded that the words of Jesus did not come from the mouth of Jesus but from the pens of the gospel writers.[1] What Matthew, Mark, Luke, and John say he said is simply that—what *they* say he said.

Yet because scholars surmise that these sayings may not have been the words of Jesus does not mean that these words are not the word of God, spoken to us who believe. Nor does it mean that these words attributed to Jesus from the cross should not be translated in the life-work of all of us who claim that we are trying to make those gospels live in our own words and lives.[2]

All these thoughts about the recounting of those words — according to Matthew, Mark, Luke, and John — and their translation in the lives of each of us reveal that there are four levels of interpretation or meaning that must concern us as we read this book. Most of us have spent time reflecting on the first level: the literal level of the actual words and deeds of Jesus. The second level proceeds from his death. Form-critics spend much time at this level. It's much like what happens among us after the funeral of a loved one, when we tell stories of the beloved and pass them on. These stories get interpreted, told and retold. And they become altered and expanded with each telling.

Decades after the Golgotha event, the stories have been worked into theologies. It's forty years with Mark, fifty with Matthew and Luke, and a good sixty or even eighty with John. This period represents the third level: the gospel *according to* Mark, Matthew, Luke, and John. The oral is now organized, and the passion is printed into gospel portraits. These gospel portraits or narratives, which contain our main source of information about the events at Golgotha, are not historical in the way we use that term today.

What really happened and what Jesus really said have been retold, rearranged, and edited to reflect the goals of the individual evangelist. These goals were theological as well as political; just putting the various gospel accounts side by side makes this clear.[3] Some scholars insist interpretation ends here, at the third level, with the words entrusted to paper, in the book we call the Bible.

But many times the words in the Bible never touch our lives. Sandra Schneiders says it well: "Historical critical work on the New Testament was rigorous in method, enticing in its possibilities, and amazingly illuminating in its results. But it seemed limited to answering questions about the first century. Somehow, though nearly infinite regress toward and beyond Christian origins seemed possible, methodologically justified progress from the text into the present of lived experience seemed impossible.''[4] But need it be so?

This "present of lived experience" represents the fourth and most important level of interpretation. This is where the scriptures and the words from the cross are to be fulfilled:

> in us,
> in our hearing,
> in our hearts,
> in our cross words and double-crosses,
> in our crosses
> where we do the nailing
> and get nailed ourselves.

It is not so much that the words are fulfilled in us as that the Word is enfleshed in us. It is not so much that those "seven last words" are translated in our lives as that the Word transforms us into those words.

At prayer one day a couple of years ago one of the brothers said, "In virtue of the word-become-flesh, we no longer know where God ends and we begin." By virtue of the death and resurrection of the Word-made-flesh, and those words enfleshed in the seven statements, the world should no longer be able to tell where Jesus' words end and our engendering of those words in our lives begins.

The goal I have in writing this book is that each of us might become the final translation, the translation that must take place in our culture, which has anesthetized and professionalized religion many layers away from the cross. Because the words from the cross and their drama continually are spoken to those who have ears to hear today, their translation in our lives cannot be a dream.

I was giving a parish retreat in the Los Angeles area when the United Nations-sponsored Truth Commission issued its report

on El Salvador's civil war of the 1980s and early 1990s. This war was funded by millions of dollars from the U.S. government. The report noted that during the twelve-year period the Salvadoran military and its government had been responsible for 85 percent of the twenty-two thousand atrocities the commission had examined.

I have been to El Salvador only once. But I had been involved in efforts to keep the Immigration and Naturalization Service from deporting El Salvadoran refugees. I also was a strong supporter of the Sanctuary Movement for refugees. Although my El Salvadoran ties were quite limited, they appeared significant enough for the FBI to investigate me and projects I helped organize. It seems these efforts to save lives were considered subversive.[5]

As I read the Los Angeles Times report, and then read about the Salvadoran president's request for amnesty—for amnesia, for forgetting about what was done and by whom—I thought of Jesus' words requesting amnesty and how they now were being applied at the fourth level of our contemporary life. But I wondered not about our Savior's motivation, but that of the El Salvadoran president.

We can apply Jesus' words not only to individuals but to our society as well. A political cartoon by Paul Conrad, published the same day as the U.N. report, illustrates that clearly. The cartoon shows Lady Liberty in the position of Michelangelo's Mary in the Pieta, crowned with the crown she wears on Liberty Island. As she holds the dead Jesus in her lap, she also holds in her hands—instead of the invitation to "give me your tired, your poor . . . "—a tablet with the words "U.S. involvement in El Salvador" (see the cartoon, which is reprinted on page 8). That cartoon by Conrad convinced me that I had to use art in this book to help me interpret how the words of Jesus on the cross speak to our culture and its crucified ones today.

When Robert Ellsberg at Orbis Books asked me to write this book of Jesus' words from the cross, I thought it would be helpful if I could share the pictures I have collected over the years. Some of these images may shock and even scandalize. Some people may think they are sacrilegious for having politics invade the profound. Others may think some boundary between the sacred and the profane has been trespassed. The intent, however, is to violate only those ways that have isolated the death of Jesus to a cross outside Jerusalem nineteen hundred years ago rather than to find, as Sebastian Moore's book title indicates for us today, that The Crucified Jesus Is No Stranger. *Indeed, as Xavier John Seubert notes,*

> *This is the insight of the contemporary depictions of the crucifixion: Jesus' humanity and all the death of humanity to which he is connected has woven into the fiber of its death the same power that raised Jesus from the dead.*[6]

Each chapter in this book has three parts. The first offers a brief personal experience or application to set the context for the particular "word." The second develops an exegetical interpretation that merges the first three levels of meaning with the fourth level, with our lives. Thus the approach I use to the exegesis is personalized. The final part of each chapter offers an art form of the cross to help us struggle with our own translation of the words into our lives so that the passage might touch us and, through us, our reality and culture.

As the third section of each of the "words" develops, I hope the reader will recognize a sevenfold progression that applies the "words" from the cross to our reality:
* *the crisis of religion and its irrelevancy to the culture;*
* *the crisis of groups when we are perpetrators of abuse;*
* *the crisis in our lives as church people when we no longer have any higher power than ourselves;*

- *the core call to conversion that comes when we surrender to God and are embraced by God's hands;*
- *the call to become communities of beloved disciples where we take Mary and each other "home";*
- *the call to let the scriptures become fulfilled in our lives;*
- *the call to fulfill the work begun by God and Jesus.*

Let us, then, take up our cross, listen to the voices speaking to us from and in this cross, listen also to those crucified today, and continue the work entrusted to us.

~ 1 ~

My God, My God, Why Have You Forsaken Me?

It was nine o'clock in the morning when they crucified him. The inscription of the charge against him read, "The King of the Jews." And with him they crucified two bandits, one on his right and one on his left. Those who passed by derided him, shaking their heads and saying, "Aha! You who would destroy the temple and build it in three days, save yourself, and come down from the cross!" In the same way the chief priests, along with the scribes, were also mocking him among themselves and saying, "He saved others; he cannot save himself. Let the Messiah, the King of Israel, come down from the cross now, so that we may see and believe." Those who where crucified with him also taunted him.

When it was noon, darkness came over the whole land until three in the afternoon. At three o'clock Jesus cried out with a loud voice, "Eloi, Eloi, lema sabachthani?" which means, "My God, my God, why have you forsaken me?" When some of the bystanders heard it, they said, "Listen, he is calling for Elijah." And someone ran, filled a sponge with sour wine, put it on a stick, and gave it to him to drink, saying, "Wait, let us see whether Elijah will come to take him down." Then Jesus gave a loud cry and breathed his last. And the curtain of the temple was torn in two, from top to bottom. Now when the centurion, who stood facing him, saw that in this way he breathed his last, he said, "Truly this man was God's Son!"

During my work on this book I found myself caught in some of the most serious conflicts of my life. Some members of my Franciscan family who were connected to our high-school seminary were publicly accused of pedophilia. During this time, in response to an issue I had raised privately with provincial leaders, I was publicly accused by those leaders of being disloyal, insensitive, in effect, an enemy. Looking back, I can understand why they may have felt that way about me. Nevertheless, their reaction, and the public humiliation, stung deeply. To compound the string of events, I was called "demonic" in The Wanderer,[1] *a paper which purports to uphold Catholicism. Statements I had made were taken out of context and no reporter asked if they were true. Believing what they read, its readers followed me wherever I went to protect others from the likes of me and to save their church from my sins. Finally, I was accused of that very sin which has become a sign of the greatest abuse of our innocents. My accusers said they had "proof" of my sin. All I could respond was that, if they did, they should indeed go to the officials and put me in jail. The accusations stopped, yet much damage had been done to my reputation.*

This barrage of rejection and condemnation created deep pain and self-doubt (to say nothing of many hours with a therapist and a spiritual director). The dynamics involved—on the part of others and on my own part—led me to grieve deeply over my own brokenness and others' betrayals, over my church and the abuse of power within it.

On the night The Milwaukee Journal *carried its first banner headline about pedophilia at our seminary—Mount Calvary, named for the Wisconsin hill where it stands — the shame I thought I had successfully addressed overtook me again. The sins of the family are visited upon each of us; I again took in that unwelcome visitor named shame. That night of darkness someone said to me — and rightly so — "Mount Calvary has become your Calvary."*

Embarrassed and feeling naked and exposed, not knowing what to do, or where to go, I looked for someone to comfort me. There was none whom I would call friend. There was no one there awake. I sat at my desk, my head in my hands, wondering why no one was there when I needed someone to know of my betrayal and battering. Then I thought how Jesus said in his betrayals, "My God, my God, why have you forsaken me?"

That night, despite my sense of abandonment and betrayal, of crucifixion, I was also able to sense a hope arising from a deeper trust. I found I still could say "My God." My own need found great consolation in the words of Jesus from the cross. In his hour of need, when he experienced abandonment, he still could say "My God."

According to Matthew and Mark, "My God, My God, why have you forsaken me" are the only words Jesus spoke from the cross. Matthew's recollection of these first words is virtually identical to Mark's. Mark says, "It was at the ninth hour"; Matthew recalls it being "about" that time that Jesus cried out with a loud voice: "Eloi, Eloi, lema sabachthani?"

In the two accounts those standing by reacted differently. Mark has the same one who ran for the vinegar-filled sponge saying: "Wait, let us see whether Elijah will come to take him down." Matthew's gospel says it was "one of them" who ran for that vinegared sponge, and it was "others" who said the same thing. But before he drank of it, death came to satisfy his thirst. "And," finally, according to Mark, "Jesus uttered a loud cry, and breathed his last." "And," Matthew recalls, "Jesus cried again with a loud voice and yielded up his spirit."

If prayer is, as our old catechism taught us, "lifting up our mind and heart to God," certainly when Jesus said, "My God, my God, why have you forsaken me?," his words were prayer. When Jesus prayed to his God, he always said *"Abba,"* except this time. Joachim Jeremias writes: *"Abbá* was an everyday word, a homely family-word, a secular word, the tender address of the child to its father: 'Dear Father.' No Jew would have dared to address God in this manner. Jesus did it always, in all his prayers which are handed down to us, with one single exception, the cry from the cross: 'My God, my God, why hast thou forsaken me?' "[2] There was no familiarity on the cross; just forsakenness, just the sense of the Father being absent from the Son. If he was to be like us in all things, he too had to move from the familiar to the formal, to the fear, to feeling forsaken. The darkness enveloping the world had to sear his senses and his soul if the terror of feeling abandoned was to be transformed into the trust of being faithful to the will of his God.

One of Mark's dominant themes is that all of Jesus' supporters gradually abandon him: first his family, then those among whom he lived, and, finally, his disciples (Mk 3:19-35; 6:1-6; 14:43-46,50,66-72). Gerard Rosse writes:

> From the beginning Jesus is presented in a progressive state of denudation and loneliness. Now, during the agony in the garden of Gethsemane the disciples sleep (Mk 14:37), then abandon him fleeing (Mk 14:50); and Peter denies him publicly (Mk 14:54ff). Even the crowd withdraws from him; it mocks him beneath the cross together with the religious authorities of Israel and the evildoers (Mk 15:29ff). Deprived now even of his gar-

ments—which underscores his loneliness even more—the Crucified is completely abandoned.[3]

On the cross the fear of the unfathomable took over from what had begun in that place called Gethsemane hours before, when he said to his disciples: "I am deeply grieved, even to death" (Mk 14:34) and then "threw himself on the ground and prayed that, if it were possible, the hour might pass from him" that was at hand. Then he said, not once but twice: "*Abba*, Father, for you all things are possible; remove this cup from me; yet, not what I want but what you want" (Mk 14:35-36,39).

I have upset people by saying that God did not want Jesus to die on the cross. Rather, God sent Jesus to be faithful among unfaithful people whose goals were not in harmony with God's. It would be deicide to think otherwise. All God wanted of Jesus was his fidelity among a faithless people, his obedience among those who were hardhearted.

Mark shows how Jesus' fidelity and obedience in such an inhospitable climate make the cross all the more imminent for him, and for all who would follow him (in whatever age that might take place).

Commitment to God's will began, for Jesus, in his ministry, after being driven by the Spirit into that first place of desert and abandonment to be tempted by Satan among the wild beasts (Mk 1:12). His ministry announced a time of fulfillment, a time of God's reign revealed in countless healings of those estranged by the system—forgiving sins in a manner the scribes considered blasphemous, associating with those abandoned by the system, and interpreting the law in ways that would meet human needs rather than their leaders' positions and propositions. The result, Mark tells us, was that "the Pharisees went out and immediately took counsel with the Herodians against him to put him to death" (Mk 3:6).

From the very beginning of Mark, Jesus prepares for the end. "The time is fulfilled," he says (Mk 1:15). Mark's gospel becomes one long introduction to his death at the hands of a system that would not accept his life and thus took judgment on itself.

Jesus knew the consequence of his actions. Not once, not twice, but *three* times, Mark's Jesus told his disciples what would happen to him and where: "Behold, we are going up to Jerusalem, and the Son of Man will be handed over to the chief priests and the scribes, and they will condemn him to death and hand him over to the Gentiles who will mock him, spit upon him, scourge him, and put him to death" (Mk 10:33-34).

When the time was up, when the hour finally did arrive for Jesus, what seemed so inevitable, so predictable, so clear became quite confusing and terrifying. Mark's Jesus learned that the hard way—through Gethsemane and Golgotha.

Somewhere between Gethsemane and Golgotha, *Abba* had become absent. The familiar now could only be formal. The darkness that came over the whole land now came inside, to take over his heart: "My God, my God, *why*?"

Why do Mark and Matthew recall Jesus' sense of being abandoned by God and not their counterparts Luke and John? Maybe it is because this passage makes Jesus on that cross so human, so agonized, so much in the depths of despair. Gods don't "cry with a loud voice"; gods don't experience abandonment; gods don't utter their agony again and again. Yet that is exactly what Mark's Jesus did on his cross—he uttered a loud cry. How ungodly of him! How human! He entered into his "why" and it entered into him. He died without an answer.

Why would Mark, followed by Matthew, make Jesus so human on that cross? Probably because that's Mark's style: unsophisticated, unpoliticized, free of ideology. He simply presents the raw Jesus on his cross. In fact, that's the Jesus we find throughout Mark's gospel. His bare emotions seem almost too human for Matthew, and even more so for Luke. John, of course, wouldn't conceive of such a human way to interpret his incarnated word. We need a more divine human for our God.

Mark's Jesus gives stern orders and commands, throws angry looks, grieves at peoples' hardness of heart, makes cynical remarks, sighs in resignation to his God as well as in frustration at his opponents, and feels stress in the midst of conflict (Mk 1:43; 3:5,12; 6:6; 7:27,34; 8:12,33; 9:19; 14:33). Like us, Mark's Jesus also does peculiar things, now and then. For instance, he took aside a deaf man with an impediment "and put his fingers into his ears"—strange enough, I'd say—but then "he spat and touched his tongue," which sounds even more strange (Mk 7:31-37). The strangeness continued as he spat on the eyes of the blind man (Mk 8:31). This was Mark's messiah! Mark's good news is free from Matthew's subtle synapses, John's sacred silences, and Luke's sanitizations. In Mark we get a Jesus, quite possibly, "just as he was" (Mk 4:36c). He spoke plainly in a way that amazed even his disciples.

If Jesus amazed his disciples, his behavior seems to have been downright scandalous to his family, who had other expectations of what it meant to be a messiah. In a passage found only in Mark—maybe because Matthew and Luke were unable to have a messiah so controversial to his own family—Jesus "went home; and the crowd came together again, so that they could not even eat. When his family heard it, they went out to restrain him, for people were saying, 'He has gone out of his mind' " (Mk 3:19b-21). One would have to be out of one's mind, it would seem, to ask God "Why?" So why did Mark's Jesus ask that question, unanswered until beyond his death?

In Mark's mind (as well as Matthew's), it was not surprising that in the rawness and nakedness of the cross Jesus cried out with a loud voice not once but twice, that Jesus asked why and felt abandoned. Maybe the difference between Mark's Jesus and our own is that his Jesus didn't run from the cross or its questions. His Jesus let himself ask the question. He not only lived with the question, he entered into it. And that's a big difference between Jesus and us. Many of us can't live with the question; we've got to be in control and have answers to any questions that might arise. But in Mark, Jesus died with the question on his lips, the question he wasn't afraid to ask. The answer to the question only came later.

The first time that raw cry defined the depth of his desolation and abandonment: "My God, my God, why have you forsaken me?" The second time the cry was the context for his death itself. Why does Luke say Jesus *uttered* his cry of dereliction with a loud voice, while Mark (and Matthew) have him *cry* his cry with a loud voice? We can only conclude that Luke seems compelled to make things look more clean on the cross than they probably were.

Luke seems to have been offended[4] that any Christ could cry with such a loud voice and then say "Why have you forsaken me?" So he had to tone things down. Those words are too human sounding, too complaining, too much the way we sound when we are forced to take up our cross — or when we "get nailed."

Apologists for Jesus seem shocked for the same reasons today. Some are uncomfortable with the tone of his voice. Others don't think a person like Jesus — who, after all, was/is God — could ask "why" or utter such a raw cry of abandonment, distrust, even dereliction. Others insist that while Jesus *might* have said these words, deeper still, so much deeper still, he really "had" the beatific vision (as though one who *is* the beatific vision can "have" it)!

This cry from the depths of desolation, the apologists tell us, proclaims the first lines of the prayer psalmists spoke centuries past and generations have prayed centuries since:

> My God, my God, why have your forsaken me?
> Why are you so far from helping me,
> from the words of my groaning?
> O my God, I cry by day, but you do not
>   answer;
> and by night, but find no rest (Ps 22:1-2).

Then they go on to say that if you read the whole psalm it testifies to a deep trust that arose from his despair. The psalm is certainly "a perfect example of the lament form" of prayer, "first portraying the desolation of the suffering Just One" in verses 1-21, "and then the triumphant vindication of the believer as God responds to his faithful one" in verses 22-32.[5] But, if crucifixion leads to asphyxiation, it is difficult to imagine how the Crucified One could have had enough breath even to say as much as Mark and Matthew record, to say nothing of a whole psalm. Moreso, to concentrate on the scandal of the abandonment may be to forget the initial scandal of the cross and a crucified God. The scandal that needs to be sanitized is not *what* Jesus said on the cross but *why* Jesus should be on the cross in the first place.

The major drama of the cross is not the scandal of Jesus feeling abandoned, but the salvation he felt in being able to say with that sense of abandonment, "My God, My God."

Apologists and exegetes sometimes forget the "My God, my God," which follows the loud cry and its sense of abandonment. And that cry makes all the difference in the world, for indeed, the event that followed has remade our world.

The "My God" cry of abandonment and desolation came from the depths of Jesus' heart where he found his God. When Jesus said, "Why have you forsaken me?," his question reveals a person traumatized in bleakness. However, when he prefaced his question with "*My* God, *my* God," any desolation or distrust was clearly grounded in familiarity and intimacy.

Ethelbert Stauffer explains that while the psalm-prayer of Jesus on the cross reveals his "inferno of dereliction" uttered "with full and final force," this cry "is no longer a crying to God for help and recompense; it is a crying after God." For Stauffer, Jesus' cry "finds its deepest meaning in prayer," and this prayer "finds its extreme expression in the cry of the dying Christ for God—a cry in which a new relationship to God, a new form of being, is already intimated."[6]

As I reflect on my own experiences of abandonment and

alienation, including times I've felt estranged from God, I have come to conclude that a major reason Jesus uttered his cry of abandonment had little to do with God. His feeling of being abandoned by God can be found somewhere else: in the friends who abandoned him. If it is true that God approaches us through others, then those others who were far away made God seem absent too. Here, at the end, at the scene of abandonment, it is as at the beginning: the temptation in the desert among the wild beasts, only now they had become passers-by and priests, a bandit and scribes who abused him. Within this temptation to come down from the cross so they could see and believe, he, who couldn't see why, still believed in the God that he didn't experience as being there. While Jesus felt God's absence in his abandonment, he believed in God's presence in his unconditional faith. And this too has made all the difference in the world. That he felt abandoned is understandable; that he *believed* he was abandoned would be unthinkable.

Mark and Matthew tell us, in their own ways, that when those around Jesus heard him call "Eli," they thought he was "calling for Elijah" (Matt 27:47; Mk 15:35). Sour wine was secured, but before it could be given to him, "Jesus gave a loud cry and breathed his last" (Mk 15:37; par. Matt 27:50). At that, Mark and Matthew say, "the curtain of the temple was torn in two, from top to bottom" (Mk 15:38; Matt 27:51). Matthew also adds an earthquake.

Because of a faith within the darkness, the most unlikely person could begin to see: "Truly," the centurion—the outsider—now said, "this man was the Son of God" (Mk 15:39). In Jesus' darkness the centurion saw; in Jesus' questioning, the centurion found meaning; in Jesus' abandonment, the centurion came to believe. He became the first of many who would know, in their darkness and abandonment, that Jesus had come to serve in a way that would ransom them and many more.

Many scholars from the second century and later thought that Mark wrote in Italy after Peter's death in Rome to a community based in or around there.[7] More recently, a growing number place Mark's redaction in or near northern Palestine.[8] Despite the place written or community addressed, it is clear that crisis and conflict, tensions and traumas, characterize Mark's gospel.

According to John Donahue, Mark's principal purpose in writing his gospel, especially its passion narrative, which flowed from the trial, was to provide a model for members of the early church being tried for their faith in the context of the Roman-Judean War (66-70 c.e.): "We suggest that Mark composes a trial of Jesus precisely as trial to meet the experiences and demands of the community for which he was writing, a community caught up in the civil strife and trials in the years during and immediately following the Jewish War."[9] What Donahue and more recent authors seem to be saying is that the main reason Mark sculpted his narrative of Jesus' trial and his story of his subsequent crucifixion was to comfort and challenge his own community thirty years later. He sought to provide in that narrative story and in the words and deeds of Jesus it described, comfort and challenge in a particular social setting of crisis and conflict, tensions and trauma.

Mark's mission continues for us today. The question confronting his community remains as a challenge for us as well: How do we find in Jesus' words—"My God, my God, why have you forsaken me?"—a message for our lives, a response to our times? How do we, caught up in our own civil, ethnic, and racial strife and our own twentieth-century trials, find comfort and challenge in Jesus' question of his God?

Mark's community was confronted with troublesome times in those "years during and immediately following the Jewish war," and we have our own problems in this period following the end of the Cold War. Ched Myers has shown that the crucifixion of Jesus cannot be divorced from "its true signification: the political theater of imperial triumph."[10] But, with the Jewish leaders as lackeys of Rome, the interests of both groups combined in what they hoped would be the triumph of church and state. If we are to be faithful, however, to the message of Mark and to its challenge, we must ask ourselves as Christians living in our own imperium, in this capitalist state, whether we are the ones who have abandoned Jesus in our pursuit of comfort and security. His words should challenge us anew: "My God, my God, why have you forsaken me?"

I was confronted with this challenge as early as the summer of 1967 at the World's Fair in Montreal. I remember only three things from my time with my family there.

First, we visited the Canadian pavilion, where we were enveloped in Canada at a movie-in-the-round. It ended with the entire darkened room singing "O Canada!" The experience was so compelling that French-speaking and English-speaking enemies by culture joined hands.

Then, in one section of the Dutch pavilion, I listened for the first time to stereophonic sound. Sitting in the booth with Philips Electronics earphones a tad away from my ears I entered a world I had never heard before.

Finally, in that same Dutch pavilion, I faced a disconcerting challenge. At a photographic exhibit on religion in the Dutch culture, giant black-and-white photos depicted scenes of Dutch life. Below the pictures scripture passages drew poignant connections between religion and culture.

One picture stood out: a flea market in Amsterdam. A huge church, double-steepled, loomed in the background. It was fronted by a flea market with merchants about their business in front of the temple. In front of the church and the market was a lifesize corpus of the dying Christ, perhaps from some church redecorated to meet the latest liturgical sensibilities. It

lay in a huge can by itself, abandoned, cast-off, thrown-away, for sale or trade or barter to the best bidder or maybe for recycling. Our imperium had found a new way to crucify: ignorance. Beneath the picture were the words "My God, my God, why have you forsaken me?"

The picture cried out the lurid triumph of the market over the message, of the culture over the cult. The ideology of buying and selling made desolate the faith about that pearl of great price for which he gave his life at the hands of others who could not see. They were too busy about buying and selling their power and prestige—all in the name of God.

Being myself a good member of my culture, I told the Dutch High Commissioner at the pavilion that I wanted to buy the picture. Months later it arrived. Rejoicing at my find, I hung it on my wall to challenge me continually about the need to understand how Christ is thrown in the garbage by our abandonment of him and his message in our lives, families, church, and culture.

How shocked I was, how my sensibilities were jarred by that picture. When I first saw it I lamented about how depraved and deprived and abandoned the Dutch church had become. But then, less than five years later, we had our own flea market.

In the early seventies our parish was changing from white to black, and the school was losing both numbers and money. We were in financial straits. So we challenged the parishes and convents and monasteries to give to us, in the name of the poor, their old altar fixtures, reliquaries, processional paraphernalia, and statues—even life-sized ones—to raise money for our school.

I used to brag that in three hours we raised seventeen thousand dollars. That was big money in the early '70s. But the dollar exacted its price. I never realized that Amsterdam's flea market had taken over St. Elizabeth's gym. And quite possibly drowning out the invitation of the auctioneer was the cry: "My God, my God, why have you forsaken me?"

I know it can be argued that those items no longer had meaning for some and could give meaning to others. I know people will say: "What you did should be done by every church, including the Vatican: selling what you have and giving it to the poor." I know still others will claim selling the items not only helped the poor, but buying the items also helped others religiously. And, in their own ways, all these statements have an element of truth. But all I know now is that there was a market mentality that made those icons a little less meaningful that day. And that day, for me, I heard a little less clearly the words: "My God, my God, why have you forsaken me?"

While I was writing this chapter, Time *magazine featured on its cover a cross in collage with the title "The Generation that Forgot God." From top to bottom were images that captured the sixties and seventies: the first man in space, the famous execution of a Vietnamese guerrilla during the Tet offensive, the Bomb, the black athletes at Mexico City on the Olympic stands giving Black Power salutes, Jackie Kennedy trying to crawl out the back of the limousine that held her dying husband, bejeweled fingers using a rolled-up dollar bill to sniff cocaine, and Richard Nixon looking so resolute and right. On the crossbeam were other images, from left to right: Woodstock, Dustin Hoffman looking at Anne Bancroft put on her nylons in* The Graduate, *the Bomb again, and finally, Jane Fonda and Michael Milken. One square in that collaged cross summed up how I have evolved into my own kind of abandonment, the way I've allowed material matters to medicate my pain, my own feelings of abandonment, and my need to be relieved of that pain and those feelings so I can come down from the cross. That square was the one with the scene from* The Graduate.

I saw the movie for the first time in downtown Milwaukee in 1968 or 1969. I had just gotten out of the seminary. Hidden in the woods of central Wisconsin, I hadn't seen a feature movie in a movie theater since Ben Hur *in the novitiate almost ten years before. So when I saw Dustin Hoffman hesitantly and gingerly but firmly put his hand on Anne Bancroft's breast I was shocked. A young couple was sitting a few rows in front of me, and my first reaction after my own shock was, "How can anyone who cares about a young woman bring her to a movie like this?"*

Over the years I've seen more scenes like that than I like to admit. They have been played out in more places than movie screens. Studs on television sells casual sex and we are not even shocked. A movie with no sex scenes is almost disappointing. Gradually our psyche gets numb and moral relativism takes over. I should know; it has happened to me. Over the decades my initial shock has been sedated into a psychic numbing that all but drowns out the words: "My God, my God, why have you forsaken me?"

What has taken place in many of our hearts has taken over the soul of the culture as well, it seems, at least according to Time. *Our theology has become therapeutic, and our journey to Gethsemane and Golgotha has become mapped to meet our needs and to take us along the path of least resistance. As a people we have come to the point of paying money to listen to a former traveling evangelist turned "loud and bawdy stand-up comic" perform "with his profane, blunt and loudmouthed stage character who screamed his way through . . . Christ's last words."*[11]

In its cover story Time *related the story of "the Walceks" in Placentia, California. The Walcek's nine children went to Mass every single morning, and said their grace before every single meal, and went to school at St. Joseph's. The children went on their own spiritual journeys in and out of Catholicism.* Time described them as not atypical of America's search for God on its own terms:

> Today, a quiet revolution is taking place that is changing not only the religious habits of millions of American[s] but the way churches go about recruiting members to keep their doors open. Increasing numbers of baby boomers who left the fold years ago are turning religious again, but many are traveling from church to church or faith to faith, sampling creeds, shopping for a custom-made God.[12]

What Time seems to be saying is that people in our consumer culture are consuming religion as long as it satisfies their desires and needs. In other words, these "shopping cart Christians" bring the individualism of the culture into their churches, and they are made to feel welcome. As long as the gospel makes no great demands on them, their need for some kind of transcendence is satisfied.

To my mind this trivialization of religion is in part a consequence of the culture's appropriation of religious symbols. Datsun saves, Datsun sets you free. And Aretha Franklin, who got her start singing gospel music in Baptist churches, sings "Deliver Me" for Pizza Hut.

Each year around Holy Week Tiffany's runs an ad in The Wall Street Journal and The New York Times advertising some kind of designer-cross. In 1984 it was Elsa Peretti's cross on a 15" eighteen-karat gold chain for $190. In 1993 it was Jean Schlumberger's cross pendant in eighteen-karat gold with cabochon rubies and a diamond for $7,500 (the chain is not included). The dollar really can't buy what it used to.

Godiva liqueurs runs a full-page ad featuring its latest creation: "The real sin would be never experiencing it," it says. Que Software says "On the 8th day, God would have created world *peace, but the PC crashed." And we know information now controls creation. "It's time to pick up the Bible," shouts a full-page ad in* The Wall Street Journal.[13] *However this "bible" doesn't even mention Matthew, Mark, and company. Rather, it refers to Exxon and General Motors, GE and IBM; and the "bible" is the Fortune 500 issue of* Fortune *magazine "on sale now." When the sacred is sold to the secular, atheism becomes theology. When consumerism invades our bodies it is not too difficult to abandon our brothers and sisters. We can easily forget that we are called not to abandon them or God in the secular, but to find them and God there.*

According to Michael Paul Gallagher, S.J., of the Pontifical Council for Dialogue with Non-believers, speaking of the brand of atheism in societies that proclaim their trust in God, "The more common form of unbelief is a cultural one," a "practical atheism," meaning that the very culture undermines the gospel. "The biggest danger to religion in the English-speaking wealthy countries," he has said, "is that the gospel becomes both passive and private. Passive in that you don't expect to make any difference in the world, and private . . . in that faith is something you keep in your heart or your soul and your relationship to God is something very hidden. So you lose out on a sense of community and you lose out on a sense of commitment." And again, as our culture's norms muffle the cross, somewhere in the distance we hear the words "My God, my God, why have you forsaken me?"

~ 2 ~

Father, Forgive Them,
for They Do Not Know
What They Are Doing

Two others also, who were criminals, were led away to be
put to death with him. When they came to the place that
is called The Skull, they crucified Jesus there with the criminals, one on his right and one on his left. [Then Jesus said,
"Father, forgive them; for they do not know what they are
doing."] And they cast lots to divide his clothing.

The other day in The Wall Street Journal *I read that the average
American is really a criminal. Though we usually don't get
caught, "we are a nation of lawbreakers. We exaggerate tax-
deductible expenses, lie to customs officials, bet on card games
and sports events, disregard jury notices, drive while intoxi-
cated — and hire illegal child-care workers. . . . Nearly all people
violate some laws, and many people run afoul of dozens without ever being considered, or considering themselves, criminals." Indeed, the two authors of the article admitted that,
between them, they had committed crimes that carried maxi-
mum jail time of fifteen years and fines of as much as thirty
thousand dollars.*[1]

29

Maybe it's because we are the criminals who don't get caught that we can be very forgiving of ourselves. Depending on what has been done, to whom, and by whom, forgiveness is forthcoming with varying degrees of difficulty. When we sin against others, and they forgive us, it is because they discover we really don't know what we are doing.

My mother had a knack for that. I wasn't even a petty criminal in the legal sense, although I had my share of brushes and near brushes with the law. I was "criminal" in the sense that, as a child, I violated parental statutes and transgressed the code of my parents and their authority. When I would do something wrong, especially as a teenager, and then regret the wrong, I would go to my mother to confess my fault and ask forgiveness. It might be that I had disobeyed or talked back, fought with my brothers, or got in trouble with the law. It might be that I had gotten angry and stormed out of the house or violated a curfew or said something mean-spirited. Still, whatever the infraction, whatever the sin, no matter the breach, I would go to my mother to confess my fault and ask forgiveness.

And then I would hear the same response—always the same beautiful response—"That's all right, Mike. I understand."

Since that time I have come to realize that when we really understand another, no matter how criminal the deed or who the criminal may be, we can only conclude there is really nothing to forgive.

If Jesus truly entered the human condition, and Luke makes it clear he did, then he, whose name implies forgiveness, should be the first to understand and, therefore, be the most forgiving of all.

The fact that I have experienced my mother's "That's all right, Mike. I understand," helps me to understand why Jesus under-

stood and could say to his parent, to his God-Parent, "Father, forgive them, for they do know not what they are doing."

I wonder sometimes if those early gospel writers knew what *they* were doing. For instance, it is quite accepted that Matthew and Luke both relied heavily on Mark's gospel, including his passion account. Matthew repeats Mark's account of Jesus saying, "My God, my God, why have you forsaken me." So, why didn't Luke? Why did Luke turn away from the abandonment theme? Why do Luke's apostles stand by Jesus and try to defend him (Lk 22:28,50)? Why is Luke silent about any flight on their part? In his account it even seems that they are present at the cross (Lk 23:49).

We already know that the answer won't be found by asking the historical question whether or not Jesus said those words. A partial answer can be intimated if we ask what kind of audience was being addressed. Mark's material "does not fit because Luke has developed a new story line,"[2] which he continues in Acts of the Apostles.

Unlike Mark, who seemed to have written for a church connected to Rome and its politics; and Matthew, who seemed to have written for a church connected to wealth and its problems; Luke's audience and its culture is hard to pinpoint. It seems he was addressing the Christian world universally more than any particular community.

We've already seen that Luke tends to sanitize the more radical statements about and by Jesus in Mark. So it is not surprising that this should be the case when he recalls Jesus' words from the cross. This "second word" is a case in point. Many early manuscripts do not contain the words here attributed to Jesus: "Father, forgive them, for they do not know what they are doing." In fact, in my *Revised Standard Version* (which is closest to the Greek), those words are bracketed. This means scholars suspect these words were inserted later.

I have never been concerned about who put the words there or why. What continues to challenge me are the words themselves. I'm not concerned that, in his effort to make Jesus on the cross less human than Mark or Matthew, Luke would not have Jesus cry a cry of abandonment. But I am concerned about what Jesus meant when he said, "Father, forgive them, for they do not know what they are doing."

While the saying remains bracketed in my *Revised Standard Version*, and some claim he didn't say such a thing,[3] the words *are* consistent with what we find in Luke's gospel and in his Acts of the Apostles. Recall that in Acts the first witness to the cross and resurrection of Jesus is Stephen—who also prayed for forgiveness for his persecutors at his killing, "Lord, do not hold this sin against them" (Acts 7:60).

The world of Luke's acts of Jesus and of his apostles was marked by reciprocity of three types. First there was universal reciprocity; you did to others what they could not do for you, and you expected no return. This response was limited to immediate families, especially parents to children. Second, there was general reciprocity; you did unto others what you expected them to do for you, and they did the same. This involved one's kin and extended family. Third came limited reciprocity. You did to others what they would do to you— before they could do it. This applied to the "theys" who were defined as enemies, outside family and kin. In those days reciprocity demanded that forgiveness be limited to family and possibly kin. It was unthinkable to extend it to enemies.

In Luke's gospel we find more about forgiveness, more about God as Father, and more about this Father's forgiveness than in any other gospel. To be offspring of that heavenly Father those who believe must imitate God in the way they forgive and welcome each other in reconciliation.

It should not be surprising, then, to have Luke's Jesus reverse the reciprocity of the *lex talionis* (an "eye-for-an-eye") in his teaching on the Plain and implement it in his plea on the cross.

There Luke's Jesus asks for forgiveness for his brothers and sisters, for those who trespassed against him.

Luke is the one who tells us about the profligate son and the far-sighted father who forgives (Lk 15:11-32). Luke also tells us about the servant who did not know the master's will and got off with fewer stripes (Lk 12:48). So, it is not surprising that, from the cross, we hear the prayer of the son and servant who has nothing to be sorry about. He asks for forgiveness for those who should be sorry but don't even know they should be, because they don't know what they are doing.

Luke's Jesus begins by addressing God here as *"Pater."* He doesn't use the term *Abba*. The gospels actually have Jesus saying *"Abba"* only once, in Gethsemane when he prayed, *"Abba*, Father for you all things are possible; remove this cup from me; yet, not what I want, but what you want" (Mk 14:36). However, we saw in the last chapter with Joachim Jeremias, and here with scholars like Gerhard Kittel, that Jesus really did say here and elsewhere *Abba* instead of *Pater*. Gottfried Quell and Gottlob Schrenk echo Kittel when they write that *Abba* is "always the original of *pater* in the prayers of the gospels."[4]

But, if the final redaction has *Pater* instead of *Abba* there must be some revelatory reason why this is so. We might ask why, at this moment of intensity, Luke would have Jesus use the more formal *Pater* rather than *Abba*, which reflects Jesus' intimacy, familiarity, and confidence in God. When the gospels call God *Pater* and not *Abba*, a different set of familial relations are recalled. *Pater* stresses a father's household authority rather than his intimacy. Acknowledging and addressing one as *Pater* was to acknowledge his authority. Indeed, the father could expect the members of the household to respect and obey his will. The term *pater* implies the need of the children to do the father's will in obedience and fidelity.

If this is so, it is not surprising that Jesus, that Beloved Son in whom the heavenly one was "well-pleased" (Lk 3:22; see 9:35), spoke of his sisters and brothers as "those who hear the word of God and do it" (Lk 8:21). If we are to be children of

that heavenly one, that ultimate God-Parent, we are to listen
to that Parent's words in Jesus and put them into practice.

The most generous rationale for people not hearing the word
of God is the one Jesus used to defend his brothers and sisters:
"They do not know what they are doing." Jesus, the firstborn
son, on behalf of his brothers and sisters, asked for forgiveness
because, he said, these members of Israel, these children of the
household, did not really know or realize or understand the
ramifications of their actions. They did not know what they
were doing.

In the Jewish scriptures, sin committed by people who didn't
know what they were doing was forgiven on the Day of Atonement: "All the congregation of the Israelites shall be forgiven,
as well as the aliens residing among them, because the whole
people was involved in the error" (Num 15:26).

D. Daube has shown that Luke's redaction of Jesus' words
about forgiveness of the people who didn't know what they
were doing echoes the prayer to God of the high priest on the
Day of Atonement. "It is, therefore, fitting," J. Massyngbaerde
Ford writes, "that Luke should portray Jesus on the cross as the
new high priest on a new Day of Atonement who intercedes
at his own most traumatic hour for all sinners."[5]

Forgiveness in Luke means "to let go," "to release," "to
liberate." I like to translate Luke's notion of forgiveness as letting go of the need to control, as getting off each other's case.
Such forgiveness-in-full is found only in God. But forgiveness
by members of God's family, frail as it may be, is precisely what
brings God's forgiveness full-circle to atonement.

In "The Pater Noster as Eschatological Prayer," Raymond
Brown writes how our forgiveness of one another as brothers
and sisters, and our forgiveness by our common Father, are
both aspects of the one great gift of forgiveness itself. In effect,
it makes enemies members of one's family. By praying the
Lord's Prayer such petitioners "stand in anticipation before the
throne of God; and they request the supreme and final act of
fatherly forgiveness, even as they extend the complete and final

act of brotherly forgiveness. This forgiveness in both directions removes all obstacles to the perfect community"[6] where all our needs are met. So now, the firstborn of the family asks for forgiveness for "them," the ones who did not know what they were doing. In the language of reciprocity, they were enemies.

"They" included the Sanhedrin—the chief priests and the scribes, both of whom had been searching for a way to put Jesus to death. In addition, "they" were the officers of the Temple police and the elders who had come for Jesus where he went to pray that night on the Mount of Olives.

These were the "they's" who should have known what they were doing but, Jesus said, they didn't. There were others: "the men who were holding Jesus [who] began to mock him and beat him. *They* also blindfolded him and kept asking him, 'Prophesy! Who is it that struck you?' " (Lk 22:63).

"They" also were the higher-ups who got involved, the Pilates and Herods. Yet "they" included not just his enemies and those at enmity with each other. "They" were also followers and friends, disciples and doers, betrayers whose questions and concerns belied their loose loyalty and fair-weathered friendship. It is clear to us today (by virtue of hindsight), who needed forgiveness that day.

I once heard a woman say that she thought the key word in this saying of Jesus was *for*: "Father, forgive them *for* they do not know what they are doing." "Once I know the *for* or *because*," she said, "I understand. This *because* becomes the condition for the compassion that gets expressed in forgiveness. The *because* is the only way to understand what they did."

Ignorance cannot be pleaded for plotters. Guilelessness does not fit the guilty. Naivete falls short before "know-it-alls." Innocence rings hollow for those with power to kill and a willingness to use it. But in Luke's gospel, as well as in Acts later, it is those who do the vile deeds, who are convinced they know what they are doing, who are indeed ignorant. So it was that Peter would tell the people that they acted out of ignorance, just as their leaders had acted in putting Jesus to death on the cross

(Acts 3:17). And Paul later said the same thing of the very same people (Acts 13:27).

Maybe it is because people like them and their leaders—and we and ours—have so much self-centeredness and preoccupation with our own interests that we stumble in delusion. Maybe it is because Jesus loved us all so much, and really *has* understood us, that he could ask for forgiveness.

Remember the time Luke tells of the woman "in the city, who was a sinner?" She came to him while he was at table and, weeping, "began to bathe his feet with her tears and to dry them with her hair?" Jesus said her sins, "which were many," were forgiven. Because she had experienced such forgiveness, she was able to show great love. He then added: "But the one to whom little is forgiven, loves little" (Lk 7:37-47).

Maybe because they loved so little they needed so much forgiveness, like that for which Jesus pleaded on the cross. Maybe because they loved so little they needed forgiveness not just from Jesus' lips but from God's throne itself. In their deep soul-sickness they did not know they needed the physician. In their righteousness they did not know the soul-sinfulness that had eaten away at their hearts. Their sickness and righteousness made them think they knew what they were doing, yet made them unable to know it at all. They, above all, had to hear words seeking that atonement which alone can be borne of forgiveness: "Father, forgive them, for they do not know what they are doing."

The question remains, however, why didn't they know what they were doing when they crucified Jesus? Until we examine why they didn't know what they were doing, we short-circuit the real meaning, which René Girard notes, "is scarcely ever recognized. The commentary on this sentence implies that the desire to forgive unpardonable executioners forces Jesus to invent a somewhat trifling excuse for them that hardly conforms to the reality of the Passion."[7]

What happens with violence, when it is endemic to a culture, is that its victims become its collaborators, the abused become perpetrators. So the Jewish leaders symbolized in Herod, and the Roman leaders in Pilate, could collaborate with each other to save each other from the people by finding a scapegoat. They had degraded him, Malina and Neyrey note, "to the limits his culture can imagine."[8] Those who bear the rejection of the abusers become scapegoats. But even the scapegoating is projected onto other "thems." It is all done unconsciously with increasing complexity until the perpetrators no longer know what they are doing.

According to Girard: "The sentence that defines the unconscious persecutor" within each of us as well as our institutions and our culture "lies at the very heart of the Passion story in the gospel of Luke: 'Father, forgive them; they do not know what they are doing' (Luke 23:34)." Girard concludes:

> If we are to restore to this sentence its true savor we must recognize its almost technical role in the revelation of the scapegoat mechanism. It says something precise about men gathered together by their scapegoat. *They do not know what they are doing.* That is why they must be pardoned. This is not dictated by a persecution complex or by the desire to remove from our sight the horror of real violence. In this passage we are given the first definition of the unconscious in human history, that from which all the others originate and develop in weaker form.[9]

When we try to identify scapegoating in our own culture—our projection onto others of the image of "enemy" to avoid embracing the alien within ourselves—we need look no further than the ways we fabricate the "diabolical enemy" among others to justify our violence toward them. And, like the Jews, it is done in the name of God and country, Temple, and Rome.

At an earlier time in my life this ideology was translated as "kill a commie for Christ." Later it justified an arms race against an "evil empire." Then it became ethnic cleansing, which could never end because the cleansing of self it demanded but masked could never be exposed.

Do you remember how quickly the United States moved from seeing Saddam Hussein as one we could do business with to "the enemy," and a diabolical enemy at that? Our righteousness has a shadow; it needs a scapegoat. Theology gave way to ideology; George Bush became the moral theologian of the nation, justifying why we were right(eous) in seeking to destroy this blight from the face of the earth. And as he announced Desert Storm, he invoked the Deity to support our troops. But the other reality that got evoked in the process was that George Bush became the shadow of Saddam Hussein. In Hussein, what we tried to repress about our need to dominate became our mirror image. The persona of us as a people got unfurled in a flag used to eliminate Saddam from our psyche.

Shortly after the Gulf War I walked alone in the midst of a gallery of paintings by the 86-year-old Hans Burkhardt called "Desert Storms" at the Jack Rutberg Fine Arts Gallery in Los Angeles. Somehow his "Lime Pit" revealed the depth of the depravity that can be reached when God becomes a justification for our violence. Scapegoats can be nailed continuously to the crosses we make for them—to keep us from being crucified ourselves by our own cross of awareness and consciousness. Yet this is the only cross that sets us free.

At a time when yellow ribbons and red, white, and blue flags flew ubiquitously, Burkhardt realized how the flag was being used to perpetuate the abuse of the latest scapegoat for our own sins. To perpetuate our lifestyle we were willing to kill for oil—all in the name of freedom.

Burkhardt began his series on the day following Iraq's invasion of Kuwait and continued it throughout Operation Desert Shield and Operation Desert Storm. In one painting called "The Desert," he nailed an old Mexican crucifix on top of a painting of the flag. Into the field normally reserved for the stars, he glued a piece of old burlap. He placed additional lengths of burlap below the flag. The flag's stripes of black and white created a sensuous surface as a backdrop to the crucifix in the center.

In the picture I have chosen, called "The Lime Pit" (see page 40), Burkhardt took a fragment of an ancient crucifix, headless, and centered it in the middle of the flag with red paint stained into the black burlap. What Burkhardt has delineated, I have come to believe, is how a culture's ideology conquers theology and subjects it to its national interests.

But this triumph of ideology over theology cannot be isolated to Desert Storms or Shields. Its scapegoats get crucified whenever God is invoked to kill "the enemy," whether from Northern Ireland, the Middle East, Yugoslavia, or elsewhere.

In the name of God we justify killing the enemy unbeliever. In 1992, at a soccer field in Bosnia, Serb guards tortured a Muslim cleric in front of a crowd. Guards ordered Imam Mustafa Mojkanovic to cross himself as a Christian. When he refused, they beat him, stuffed his mouth with sawdust and beer, then slit his throat.[10] All this probably was done in the name of the lamb who died on that cross.

Until we realize how the one we have made our enemy is really a projection of what we hate in ourselves we will never know what we are doing and will never be able to forgive. But once we know what we have done, as Jesus on his cross knew and Stephen on the pavement knew, then we understand and then there is nothing to forgive.

If we cannot forgive, we end up crucifying ourselves on the very cross we construct for our scapegoats. Our hate will be the hatred in ourselves that we have repressed, and that hatred of others masking our own self-hatred will continue to crucify us in their name.

In 1984, Time *magazine had a cover feature called "Why Forgive?" It showed a picture of Pope John Paul II shaking hands with his would-be assassin, Mehmet Ali Agca, in what became a most powerful moment of reconciliation. However,* Time *probed more deeply, beyond the two men who had become reconciled, to the groups they represented. These groups are still in conflict because of the scapegoating that continues, claiming still more victims.*

The story of the scapegoating that continues to crucify, Time *showed, repeats itself in the Middle East, in Northern Ireland, in Central America, and in those terrorist acts that continue to inflict wrongs on others. The alternative, Lance Morrow,* Time's *essayist noted, whether for individuals or nations, is to perish "in their own fury."*

Whether as a result of our petty arguments with each other we make enemies of friends or whether as groups and nations we scapegoat others with our "isms," Morrow's conclusions make relevant the wisdom of Jesus' words from the cross about forgiveness. Morrow writes:

> *The psychological case for forgiveness is overwhelmingly persuasive. Not to forgive is to be imprisoned by the past, by old grievances that do not permit life to proceed with new business. Not to forgive is to yield oneself to another's control. If one does not forgive, then one is controlled by the other's initiatives and is locked into a sequence of act and response, of outrage and revenge, tit for tat, escalating always. The present is endlessly overwhelmed and*

*devoured by the past. . . . Not to forgive is to be impris-
oned by our projections, to be enslaved by our own scapegoating, to be victims of our violence, to be abused by our
abuse. . . . Forgiveness frees the forgiver. It extracts the
forgiver from someone else's nightmare.*[11]

By praying for his enemies Jesus redefined reciprocity to include
all as brothers and sisters. When Jesus prayed "Father, forgive
them, for they do not know what they are doing," the scapegoat
became the Lamb who took away the sin of the world.

He extracted himself from the nightmare of the world. The only
way to be free of the repression—self-imposed, taken in from
others—will come when we too can forgive ourselves and our
"thems." The crucifixions can end with us. The scapegoating
need find no more victims or perpetrators in us. It all begins
when we too can say "Father, forgive them, for they do not
know what they are doing."

~ 3 ~

Today You Will Be
with Me in Paradise

Two others also, who were criminals, were led away to be
put to death with him. When they came to the place that
is called The Skull, they crucified Jesus there with the criminals, one on his right and one on his left. ... And the
people stood by, watching; but the leaders scoffed at him,
saying, "He saved others; let him save himself if he is the
Messiah of God, his chosen one!" The soldiers also mocked
him, coming up and offering him sour wine, and saying, "If
you are the King of the Jews, save yourself!" There was also
an inscription over him, "This is the King of the Jews."

One of the criminals who were hanged there kept deriding him and saying, "Are you not the Messiah? Save yourself
and us!" But the other rebuked him, saying, "Do you not
fear God, since you are under the same sentence of condemnation? And we indeed have been condemned justly,
for we are getting what we deserve for our deeds, but this
man has done nothing wrong." Then he said, "Jesus,
remember me when you come into your kingdom." He
replied, "Truly I tell you, today you will be with me in
Paradise."

*I once used a riddle in speaking to young people so they could
figure out where I lived at St. Benedict's Friary in downtown*

Milwaukee. I said: "I live across the street from hundreds of individuals and not one of them wants to live there. Where do they live?" After a few guesses that included an orphanage and a zoo, a fourth grader figured it out. I live across from alleged criminals, hundreds of them, consigned to jail awaiting their hearings or trials. On another side of our Friary there are scores more consigned as criminals sentenced to stay in prison to work out their sentence.

The names of those crucified with Jesus were unlisted by Matthew, Mark, Luke, and John, though Luke, for some reason, used the word kakourgoi, or "criminals" for them while Mark and Matthew call them lēstai, or "bandits." John simply says "two others." Luke has chosen to write about what happened among the crucified ones more than the other evangelists. Could he have been a prison chaplain too?!

Every Friday in our living room prison chaplains working in the jail across the street come to reflect on the scriptures for the following Sunday.

I always look forward to those sharings because the stories and applications make the scriptures come alive for me. The first, second, and third levels of scriptural interpretation find the fourth as metal filings leap to a magnet. A couple of years ago one of the criminals across the street was a man who, unlike those criminals crucified with Jesus, had a name that brought him an international reputation: Jeffrey Dahmer, the serial killer. Most of his victims were young men scapegoated by society for being gay.

If our scapegoats are the projection of repressed thoughts, feelings, and behaviors we hold within, what we reject "out there" often is repressed "in here," where our hearts are trying to be free. And so Jeffrey Dahmer, who had a repulsion for gays, was *willing to kill them to avoid facing that which was killing him within.*

But as we prayed in our living room, we discovered another dimension about Jeffrey Dahmer: he lives deep within us. The seducer of the innocent lives deeply in our fantasies and fetishes. Its shadow sneaks out in our curiosity. And when we cannot stomp out our shadow through our scapegoats, we legitimize it by reading, voyeurs that we can be, the pornographic particulars. It is not surprising, then, that when People's cover-feature on Jeffrey Dahmer hit the newsstands it became one of their biggest sellers of all time. Jeffrey Dahmer is alive not only in central Wisconsin; he's hidden but possibly quite alive in the center of our hearts.

One day the promise from Jesus on the cross to an unnamed criminal came home to me loud and clear. The morning's Milwaukee Sentinel featured the story of one of the chaplains who had been visiting Jeffrey Dahmer and his family. The headline proclaimed, "Cleric Says Dahmer Could Go to Heaven."[1] I don't know why that prediction was considered significant enough to be one of the main headlines that morning. After all, nineteen hundred years before another criminal, unnamed, condemned for an unnamed crime, heard not a prediction but a promise of a similar nature.

Jesus' promise guarantees the same to the criminal within each of us — who seeks it out — that was originally made to that criminal: "Today you will be with me in Paradise."

The Mediterranean world to which Luke seems to have written has been viewed traditionally as conflict-ridden. Hence, according to scholars like Bruce Malina and Jerome Neyrey, "it

should come as no surprise when Luke's stories of Jesus or early
Christian groups emerge as stories of conflict. It is quite significant, however, to note that Mediterranean conflict has always
been over practical means to some end, not over the ends
themselves. Jesus and the faction he recruited were in conflict
with other groups over how best to heed the command of God,
not over whether God should be obeyed at all."[2]

Over 40 percent of Luke's narration regarding Jesus on the
cross involves details about the two criminals crucified with
him. Joseph Fitzmyer and E. Earle Ellis declare that this "criminal section" represents the core of Luke's crucifixion scene.
They may be a bit quick in making their judgment. However,
if we look further and link the *challenge* of the one criminal to
Jesus with the *promise* made to the other criminal by Jesus, we
discover a basic theme of Luke's entire gospel. This is the theme
of salvation.

In the midst of the crowd—which stands by silently—Luke
narrates three times how Jesus was taunted about salvation,
about saving himself *from* the cross. All three of his taunters
used the word for "to save," *sōzein*. While the first and second
taunts from the leaders and the soldiers also can be found in
Mark and Matthew, Luke added a third to construct a triad of
taunts. According to Joseph Fitzmyer, this addition "highlights
the salvific significance of Jesus' crucifixion in the Lucan Gospel: He is crucified precisely as 'Savior,' a major theme in Lucan
theology."[3]

The first time came when the leaders rejected Jesus as the
Messiah and mocked him: "He saved others; let him save himself if he is the Messiah of God, his chosen one!" (Lk 23:35).
They were joined by the soldiers, who degraded him for being
given the status of king, saying: "If you are the King of the Jews,
save yourself!" (Lk 23:37). Finally, Luke tells us, the scorn of
the leaders was echoed when "one of the criminals who was
hanged there kept deriding him and saying, 'Are you not the
Messiah? Save yourself and us!' " (Lk 23:39).

From their scoffing, their mocking, and their derision, which reflects the sparring so symptomatic of a shame-based society, these three groups reveal that they already had in mind what salvation had to mean. (In that, they probably aren't much different from us.) All three had convinced themselves that salvation meant liberation from the cross. In their confidence, they were much like the devil in the desert, who offered tempting alternatives, a seductive salvation. The leaders and soldiers demanded *if* Jesus were the messiah, and *if* Jesus were the king of the Jews, he should show it by saving himself.

It isn't that Jesus *couldn't* have been tempted in the desert or on the cross to their way of salvation. After all, what healthy person prefers pain or covets the cross? Jesus did not run to his cross. He asked to have the cup removed. But even more than believing in the One who could remove it, he wanted to be faithful. In the spirit of obedience, which constitutes the heart of salvation, he said, "Not my will but yours be done" (Lk 22:42).

Such a response did not characterize the qualities the leaders and soldiers expected of a king and messiah. Their understanding of salvation was linked with Jesus' coming *down* from the cross. Yet Luke's Jesus finds salvation *in* the cross. And this salvation summarizes the whole purpose of Jesus' presence on earth.

Jesus' actions fulfilled Isaiah's vision of salvation:

> Every valley shall be filled
> and every mountain and hill shall be made
>   low,
> and the crooked shall be made straight,
> and the rough ways made smooth;
> and all flesh shall see the salvation of God.
>   (Lk 3:5-6, quoting Isa 40)

It was the angels who had first announced "good news of great joy for all the people": salvation in the city of David, salvation in a savior, salvation in a messiah, salvation in this

Lord (Lk 2:10-11). And it was the Spirit who filled him with power, who led him, and who had come upon him to bring salvation to the poor, the captives, the blind, and the oppressed in a way that would "proclaim the year of the Lord's favor" (Lk 4:14-19).

Whether to the poor, the captives, the blind, the oppressed, people in need of his healing, women needing affirmation, strangers, or tax collectors, Jesus' salvation went beyond the offspring of Abraham and Sarah to those who accepted him on his terms. When they did this, salvation came to them and their households. Many times the recipients were people society termed losers. As Donald Senior writes in *The Passion of Jesus in the Gospel of Luke,* "The 'salvation of God' which Jesus embodies cannot be denied by boundaries of gender or time or religious propriety."[4] As Jesus declared, "The Son of Man came to seek out and to save the lost" (Lk 19:10).

When we don't know we're lost we don't know we need to be found. When we don't know we're lost we don't know we need to be saved. When we possess the way to salvation we don't know we need to be saved. Maybe that was the problem with the leaders and the soldiers with their crosses, and the criminal on his. This wasn't the case, however, with the second criminal. He recognized his need for salvation. He sensed liberation from his cross would come from Jesus on his. He intuited what Luke's Zechariah had spoken years before: that salvation would come not by coming down from a cross but by "the forgiveness of their sins" (Lk 1:77).

Salvation would come with staying on that cross to death, with the obedience and fidelity that his death represented. The Jesus who was condemned by human beings, mocked, scorned, and derided about saving himself was "saved" by God through resurrection in a way that brought salvation to the earth and its peoples.

The second criminal was the only one who seemed to realize the connection between forgiveness and salvation. He knew what he was doing when he rebuked his fellow criminal with the words: "Do you not fear God, since you are under the same sentence of condemnation? And we indeed have been condemned justly, for we are getting what we deserve for our deeds, but this man has done nothing wrong" (Lk 23:40-41). The two criminals had done enough wrong to deserve punishment. But Jesus had done nothing wrong. He is the just one condemned unjustly. The second criminal knew the difference.

In Luke's passion, fulfillment of the many passages about the "Just One" comes through the one who suffers to bring about salvation for the many. Jesus, the Just One who suffers, brings about salvation in the midst of criminals. As Richard Dillon writes: "It was the merger of this tradition with that of the Deuteronomic 'prophet of Moses' (Dt 18:155ff) that produced the celebrated song of the 'suffering servant' in Isaiah 52-53, where the 'servant,' who was 'numbered among the outlaws' (Is 53:12 = Lk 22:37), is expressly named 'the just one' who 'will make the many just' by bearing their iniquities (Is 53:11)."[5]

People who don't fear God are ignorant of their iniquities and deluded about what they are doing by their pride and self-centeredness. Such, it seems, was the case of the first criminal. But the other one looked at himself and his crime in light of the Just One crucified with him. He did not fear the soldiers and leaders who had condemned him, but the God he was about to meet. Recognizing the folly of his own deeds, of which he was very conscious, the second criminal requested forgiveness and salvation: "Jesus, remember me when you come into your kingdom" (Lk 23:42).

The criminal called him Jesus, which means "Yahweh saves." This was "the name given by the angel before he was conceived in the womb" (Lk 2:21). He recognized the reality behind the address. He admitted his need for forgiveness, for salvation from his sins. He needed Yahweh to save him, not from the wood of his cross, but from a cross that crucified him at the soul-point of his fear: "Jesus, remember me when you come into your kingdom."

In Luke's narrative, remembering can't be limited to memory. Being "mindful of" someone goes beyond the mind to the heart. In this scene "remembering" and "mindfulness" go back to salvation itself. When remembering is effective, it effects salvation.

Otto Michel notes: "Every event on earth has its 'effect' on God. His remembrance is concealed in His acts of grace and judgement. The fact that God remembers is revealed by the word of His messengers. . . . The thief on the cross, sensing the future glory of Christ, lays his fate in the hands of Jesus" — when he asks Jesus to "remember" him as he enters into his kingdom.[6]

What is Jesus' response? He didn't probe into the man's problems or his past; he didn't poke around or prod him to cleanse himself with confession. No. The first word Jesus says in response to this request from a common criminal is "Amen."

Most of our prayers to God, to Jesus, to the Spirit, don't begin with "Amen"; they end with it. We say to God what we need to say or want to express, and then say "Amen." But here on the cross, it is the other way around. Jesus' *first* response to the criminal's prayer is "Amen." He then says what he needs to say and wants to say with assurance: "I tell you, today you will be with me in Paradise."

In Luke's gospel, "Amen" is on the lips of Jesus only seven times. This is less than in any of the other gospels. But whenever that "Amen" is uttered it is followed with the declarative "I tell you," meaning that what is about to be declared will be reinforced in the heavens. Because Jesus is himself the "Amen," what he says carries with it the divine affirmation as well as its confirmation: "Amen, I tell you, today you will be with me in Paradise." The one in whom God's reign is present is now the incarnate Amen whose "Amen" confirms the reality of Paradise for the one asking to enter. Moreover, that saving entrance will be "today."

Luke's "today" is not temporal. His *sēmeron* is something special. His "today" always contains within it a promise, a message of salvation for those who hear it and hope.

"Today" in the city of David "a Savior, who is the Messiah, the Lord" was born (Lk 2:11). *"Today"* outside of the city of Jerusalem is where healing will come and his death will occur (Lk 13:32-33). As Jesus passed through the city of Jericho Jesus stayed at Zacchaeus's house and that day, which was *"today,"* salvation came to it (Lk 19:5-9). It is not surprising that outside the city of Jerusalem, Jesus should say: "Today, you will be with me in Paradise." Even more so, it is not surprising that, for all those *todays* with their signs of salvation — the crowds witnessing Jesus' signs of salvation in bodies and souls should glorify God and say in amazement as they returned to their city, *"Today* we have seen strange things" (Lk 5:26).

Another remarkable thing in Jesus' response to the criminal's cry was the part of the phrase that declared: "This day you will be *with me* in Paradise." Although he uses the phrase *"with me"* (*met emou*) only four times, when Luke's Jesus does talk about being "with him" he invariably means an exceptional kind of presence. The presence promised in Paradise represents no less than an abiding presence promised *today* to those who ask.

Paradise is not mentioned in Matthew, Mark, and John. It can be found only here in Luke. But it is what our hearts were made for and what we long for and what the criminal sought from Jesus on his cross. Thus Jesus' answer to the criminal, Joachim Jeremias says,

> Goes beyond what is asked for, for it promises the thief that already today he will enjoy fellowship with Jesus in Paradise. Paradise signifies here the place which receives the souls of the righteous departed after death. It is the hidden (intervening) Paradise. But in the eschatological *"sēmeron"* there is also expressed the *hic et nunc* of the dawn of the age of salvation. In the promise of forgiveness the "one day" becomes the "to-day" of fulfillment. Paradise is opened even to the irredeemably lost man hanging on the cross. He is promised fellowship with the

Messiah. How unlimited is the remission of sins in the age of forgiveness which has now dawned.[7]

If Paradise is the promised "place" for those who will be with Jesus, it follows that for those who have no "place" for Jesus in their lives, the possibility of Paradise becomes problematic, even questionable. Even though Joachim Jeremias talks about Paradise as a place, it more accurately represents a state, a state of being with someone in a relationship: "Today you will be *with me.*" But for those who ask, Jesus' promise becomes proclamation. The criminal on his cross that day was the first to be saved. He was canonized before he died.

Since I live across the street from those judged by society as criminals, I began to wonder just how that long-ago criminal might have heard Jesus' promise were he alive today. So, I went across the street to the jail and visited with R. S. Johnson, a man consigned to a cell for a crime I did not ask about. What I did ask was that he imagine himself on the cross that day with Jesus and what Jesus' words would mean to him. R. S. entitled his resulting portrait: "Remember me, Lord, when you come into your kingdom." He accompanied his drawing, done in pencil, with a reflective explanation:

> *Surrounding the man condemned to die, and at his right hand, stands the Judge and Lady Justice. When Lady Justice lays down her sword the balance is lost between God's law and that of humans. The Judge represents the concerns of the group who rules, whose concerns now define the rulings of Lady Justice. She has taken to herself the definitions of the society and its rulers rather than taking her sword to defend the oppressed. She has laid down her sword used to fight the battle of oppression; man has truly gained control of her.*

> *At the condemned one's left stands the guard and exe-cutioner. The black guard represents our black society. But*

I feel it is no longer a black and white issue. It's an issue of who has and has not. Many blacks with positions have taken a laid-back attitude, afraid to state their true feelings on issues of great importance. They tend not to be out-spoken, fearing what their white co-workers might think. They alone can do only so much. But I should understand. If I myself worked so hard wouldn't I be careful to do so well? Without these people to make a way, our whole effort to gain equality shall be lost.

The dead man in the lower right represents those who suffer because of official corruption at the hands of those concerned only about their own interests. When one sees the oppressed being persecuted and does nothing to cor-rect it, do you not become part of the offense as well?

There are others, however, who are guilty—the man in the orange jail garb with the dice beside his head. As a man gets caught up in his wrongs, one thing is for certain: he shall lose! Whether it be his life or the loss of ones who truly care for him, he shall lose! But the one thing that he will never lose is God's love. To be reborn, one must stop violating God's laws, represented in the skull, and be reborn in the spirit.

My family remains to be the strength of me. For they came through God as a gift to me. [The lady in prayer with the child represents R. S.'s wife and children.]

In the center of the portrait is a man condemned to die. As he is about to go into a place not known to him, he acknowledges God as his Lord and Savior. He is accepted by God and his sins are forgotten.

For people in jail, the desire for salvation is personal and pal-pable. Yet many of us who are not confined to jail cells seem *beyond acknowledging the need for any God to be our Lord, any savior to be ours. Maybe this is not because God has forgotten our sins, but because we have.*

When sin becomes relative, there is no need for salvation. When therapy explains away responsibility, we need no savior.

I recognized this kind of righteousness in myself one day when I heard Janet Sullivan, a Franciscan sister, say: "We've come a long way when we no longer think we are in need of salvation." When I heard that I realized I had come a long way indeed. I had become healthy with my brand of creation-centered spirituality; I was co-creator; I was no longer sick. But, Luke reminds us, it is only the sick who need the physician; only sinners, who know they are sinners, can be open to salvation as well as to the Savior who alone can bring it. When there's no place in our lives for salvation or the Savior, we miss the chance to be promised Paradise.

Why don't we think of ourselves as in need of salvation? Maybe it is because it seems like such a fundamentalist notion. We get turned off by those who seem so easily saved once and forever. Or maybe it seems like jargon coming from those we perceive as righteous, but who have little or no concern for the poor or justice. But I wonder too if it's not a reaction to notions of salvation which no longer work for us.

In Sin as Addiction *Patrick McCormick shows how we have experienced in our theologies various notions of sin and, with these images, different understandings of what salvation entails.*

In the first image, sin is a stain which defiles us. Salvation comes through the cleansing waters of baptism. Next, sin can be conceived as a crime that cries for punishment of the criminal. And since our crime was infinite, insofar as the criminals committed it against someone infinite, it demanded an infinite response

that only someone infinite could pay. Third, sin can be conceived not as a stain or a crime, but as a relationship that is
broken and in need of repair. Salvation comes in the one called
"repairer of the breach." For others, sin might be considered a
disease, and disease might be treated as a character flaw, a lack
of responsibility. Salvation comes in healing and liberation from
the flaws. Finally, McCormick writes, sin might be considered
an addiction, something beyond our total control, yet something for which we are ultimately responsible.

This is the notion that has come to mean much for me. But,
like all addictions, it demands that we recognize its power over
us and our need for a Higher Power to deliver us from its
control. This Higher Power comes to me in the form of Jesus
Christ. So, prisoner of my addictions, as I know I am, I find
release in the saving presence of Jesus Christ in my life. I must
find my ultimate freedom to be who I am in him or remain in
the cell of my false self.

Accepting Jesus as my Savior and the Savior of my world, I find
comfort in the prayer of R. S. Johnson:

So dear Lord Jesus, when my life is over, as I go through
this life that is so unjust, remember me when you come
into your kingdom. For I see so much wrong with this
world and yet I also see so much good. They say the best
things in life are free; surely my Lord, the Love you give is
that ultimate of all gifts. And for this I can only say, "Thank
you, Lord. Amen."

～ 4 ～

Father, into Your Hands
I Commend My Spirit

It was now about noon, and darkness came over the whole land until three in the afternoon, while the sun's light failed; and the curtain of the temple was torn in two. Then Jesus, crying with a loud voice, said, "Father, into your hands I commend my spirit." Having said this, he breathed his last. When the centurion saw what had taken place, he praised God and said, "Certainly this man was innocent." And when all the crowds who had gathered there for this spectacle saw what had taken place, they returned home, beating their breasts.

In the late 1980s I had a bad car accident. I was taken by ambulance to a hospital. I suffered a broken ankle and needed approximately thirty stitches to repair my eyelid, eyebrow, and forehead.

During the next month, with shooting pains in my chest, I finally decided I should go back to a hospital.

There I was told I either had double pneumonia or blood clots on my lung. It would be very much better for me, they said, if I had pneumonia.

As I sat in the office waiting for the doctor's return with the X-rays I had a bit of time to reflect on my future. I wondered what would come of it, what the possibility of blood clots would mean for me.

When the doctor returned with his report, I was not that surprised to hear him say, "You have blood clots on your lung and are in serious condition. If they move you might die. So you must have five days of absolute bed rest. During that time we will try to dissolve them."

Although I was not surprised at what I heard—that I might die—what did surprise me is the way I responded to the news.

It wasn't that I welcomed it. Nor did I run from it. I didn't exactly relish the thought, but it did not frighten me. I only recall thinking to myself, "That's not so bad."

That thought, I tell myself now, revealed a kind of surrender. And with that surrender I experienced an embrace. I think it was a little experience of what resurrection must mean, a promise made to be recalled when the dying begins. That little thought was my own unique way of repeating words I had heard before: "Father, into your hands I commend my spirit."

In the beginning, according to the Yahwist in Genesis, the hands of God fashioned humanity when "the Lord God formed *adam* from the dust of the ground, and breathed into his nostrils the breath of life; and the *adam* became a living being" (Gn 2:7). In the end, according to Luke's gospel, Jesus, who had had the breath of life fashion him a human in the womb of Mary, now entrusted himself into the hands of the Creator: "Father, into your hands I commend my spirit."

The words sound simple, but Luke's context makes them quite cosmic. Earlier, placing Jesus *in* Jerusalem and its Temple, Luke recalls him saying of that Temple that "all will be thrown down" and that cosmic signs "in the sun, the moon, and the stars" will "be the sign that this is about to take place" (Lk 21:6,25,7). So now, with Jesus *outside* Jerusalem and its Temple, Luke recalls—with Matthew and Mark—that "darkness came over the whole land." But then, he notes—unlike Matthew and Mark—that "the curtain of the temple was torn in two" *before* the death of Jesus.

Historicists and fundamentalists struggle with passages in the synoptics that conflict, as these do. What happened to that curtain? When? In Mark and Matthew, the curtain is "torn in two, from top to bottom" (Matt 27:51; Mk 15:38), and in Luke the "top to bottom" part is missing? Why? Why in Matthew and Mark does the tearing of the curtain happen upon Jesus' death, and in Luke precede it? Such questions indicate how the questioner forgets—as we are trying *not* to forget—that Luke's gospel is not intended to record literal history. It is the good news of Jesus *according to Luke.* So, if we are to find good news in Luke, we must probe his message about changes in the cosmos and the curtain.

Both the sun's darkening and the rending of the Temple veil point ominously to some kind of divine judgment on the land and the Temple. Joel had warned that "the sun shall be turned to darkness" before "the great and terrible day of the Lord comes" (Joel 2:30). At his arrest Luke's Jesus said, "When I was with you day after day in the temple, you did not lay hands on me. But this is your hour, and the power of darkness!" (Lk 22:53). With Jesus outside the Temple in the darkness, the fractured veil of the Temple as well as the darkness itself combined to offer a most foreboding sign.

To first-century Mediterranean minds signs of cosmic upheaval and structural cataclysms accompanied moments of great religious occurrences. Even today, many reports of apparitions of the Blessed Virgin are accompanied by accounts of the sky turning dark or the sun turning around.

The culmination of the events since the arrest reveal God's judgment on these occurrences through the darkening of the skies. It indicates the cosmic implications in Jesus' impending death (even though Luke does not refer to his social location as the "earth," but the "land" — referring to that particular spot on earth called Palestine).

Before we wonder about the rending of the Temple veil, it might be good to discuss where that veil actually hung. *Katapétasma* referred to the curtain or veil before the Holy of Holies or before the Holy Place. This prevented people from viewing the interior of the Temple. If the veil were torn in two, people could not be shut out. All who entered would have a new kind of access to the presence of God. But that was unthinkable — until the time of Jesus' death.

In Luke, Jerusalem's Temple figures prominently, from the very beginning. Jesus' first words indicate he *had* to be (*dei*) there (Lk 2:49). Mark has Jesus teaching in various places, yet Luke's Jesus teaches in the Temple. During his final time in Jerusalem, Mark's Jesus is in the Temple only three days; Luke's Jesus teaches daily in the Temple. After "cleansing" it and prophesying its destruction Jesus continued to use it (Lk 19; 21). Indeed, as Dennis Sylva argues, the Temple functions throughout Luke as a holy place. Acts tells us Jesus' followers continued to use it as well. This is not surprising. By now — at the third level of the scriptures — their allegiance had been grounded elsewhere than in a building.

No physical building would be threatened by the rending of its curtain. But the splitting of the Temple's curtain spelled "curtains" for the leadership of the chief priests who had been threatened by Jesus' challenge to their abuse of power — which they executed in the name of the Temple (and, probably, in the name of its curtain too).[1]

After the skies were darkened Jesus looked beyond the Temple. And when the Temple's curtain was torn in two, he simply said: "Father, into your hands I commend my spirit." As Eduard

Lohse points out, in the more than two hundred places in the Hebrew scriptures that speak of the "hands" of the Father-God, the reference invariably expresses God's activity in the human situation in a way that reveals God's power at work in creation. It is not surprising that after such a display of God's power at work in creation, which originated at God's *hand* (Acts 7:50; Is 66:2), Jesus would entrust his spirit into the hands of his Father. The hand(s) of God, who acted in history to intervene, to help, and to protect (Lk 1:66; see Acts 11:21) were the same hands to which Jesus could entrust his very spirit: "Into your hands I commend my spirit."

For Luke, Jesus *commending* his spirit to the hands of God involved an act of total trust. This self-donation culminated his final conversion, his final "turning over" of his life into the hands of his God—the surrender of a child in provident faith to a parent.

What Jesus "commended" to his God-Parent was his spirit. This spirit represented the core of his being.

Throughout his life, Luke represents Jesus as being under a kind of divine compulsion. This compulsion was translated as some kind of necessity or inevitability (*dei*). Of the 102 times the word or its parallel is used, 41 are found in the Lucan writings. Walter Grundmann notes:

> The term may . . . be used as a general expression for the will of God, the statement with which it is linked thereby acquiring the significance of a rule of life (Lk. 15:32; 18:1; Ac. 5:29; 20:35). Jesus sees His whole life and activity and passion under this will of God comprehended in a *dei*. Over Him there stands a *dei* which is already present in his childhood. This is the *dei* of the divine lordship (Lk. 2:49). It determines His activity (Lk. 4:43; 13:33; 19:5). It leads Him to suffering and death, but also to glory (Lk. 9:22; 17:25; 24:7, 26; Ac. 1:16; 3:21; 17:3). It has its basis in the will of God concerning Him which is laid

down in Scripture and which He unconditionally follows (Lk. 22:37; 24:44).[2]

Throughout his life, in response to this *dei*, this divine necessity, Jesus had commended his body, his direction, his ministry, his will, his whole being to his Father. Now, from the cross, he could commend his spirit, his *pneuma*, as well. This was that part of himself which would survive any death.

In Jesus' surrender of his very spirit he opened himself to be touched by the hand of his God, to enter into his God's embrace. In his words of surrender Jesus became a model of true conversion to God: "Into your hands I commend my spirit." Donald Senior writes:

> These final words of the earthly Jesus tell the full meaning of the "Son of God" title in Luke. Jesus is "son" because he is willing to entrust his entire being to God, even as death pulls at that relationship and seeks to put it into doubt. Here another allied, biblical tradition is invoked by Luke. The wisdom tradition of the suffering just one (also called "Son of God" as in Wisdom 2:13, 16, 18; 5:5) reflected on the mystery of trust under assault. This figure of the Israelite who trusts in God yet is nearly overwhelmed by suffering and isolation haunts many of the lament psalms and the early chapters of the Wisdom of Solomon. As Jesus approaches the threshold of death, he too, is mocked as the just one of Israel was (23:25-39). But his last word [according to Luke] is not despair or bitterness, but complete trust. As darkness snuffs out the light of the sun, and the veil of the temple is torn apart, Jesus, true child of God, places his battered spirit into the hands of his Father.[3]

"Into your hand I commit my spirit" was part of the psalm prayed by Israel's sons and daughters for centuries. Psalm 31

was a night prayer. Now, on the cross, in the evening of his
life, it all came back to Jesus:

> In you, O Lord, I seek refuge;
> do not let me ever be put to shame;
> in your righteousness deliver me.
> Incline your ear to me; rescue me speedily.
> Be a rock of refuge for me,
> a strong fortress to save me.
> You are indeed my rock and my fortress;
> for your name's sake lead me and guide me.
> Take me out of the net that is hidden for me,
> for you are my refuge.
> Into your hand I commit my spirit;
> you have redeemed me, O Lord, faithful God.
>   (Ps 31:1-5)

In Jesus' prayerful surrender we find the archetype of the
gift of martyrdom, which lies at the heart of all self-donation
into the hands of another. This becomes crystal-clear when,
according to Luke-Acts, the protomartyr, Stephen, faced death
at the hands of his own people. Stephen's plea for his persecutors echoed Jesus' own prayer: "Lord, do not hold this sin
against them" (Acts 7:60). Similarly, Stephen's prayer while
being stoned echoed Jesus' final words as well: "Lord Jesus,
receive my spirit" (Acts 7:59). The parallels are so close that
Stephen's trial before the Sanhedrin contains material Luke
could have included in his account of Jesus' trial; namely, the
prophecy of the Temple's destruction. But even more than
presenting a model of Jesus' way of dying in Stephen's repli-
cation of his pattern, these scriptures are written that we might
make this pattern of dying our own. The first three levels finally
must be translated in the words of *our* life. Jerome Neyrey
writes:

> By dying with a prayer to God on his lips, Jesus shows the
> new covenant community the proper way to die, viz.,

with faith in God to save him from death. This is confirmed in Acts in the depiction of Stephen imitating Jesus' death. As Jesus died praying "Father, into your hands I commit my spirit," so Stephen died with a like prayer on his lips: "Lord Jesus, receive my spirit" (Acts 7:59). Inasmuch as Stephen is the first Christian martyr to die, his death is of great interest. It is pastorally significant that his death be modeled on Jesus' death. Like Jesus, he shows faith, saving faith.[4]

Having surrendered saying the psalm, Jesus embraced approaching death: "He breathed his last." Now, "when the centurion saw what had taken place," he too showed faith, possibly, a saving faith. "He praised God and said, 'Certainly this man was innocent' " (Lk 23:47).

The word Luke uses for "innocent" (*díkaios*), as the *RSV* translates it, often is translated as "just" or "righteous." While Matthew would stress the "just" dimension of the meaning of "innocent," Luke stresses the "righteous" dimension, which he often links with salvation. This seems clear from the fact that Luke narrates how the centurion first "praised" (*doxazein*) God and then said "this man was innocent" (*díkaios*). Eight of the nine times Luke uses the word for "praise," he refers to direct praise of God. In most of these places, however, the reason for peoples' praise of God stems from salvific activity on the part of Jesus. In other words, as Matera notes,

> People give glory to God when God manifests his salvific activity in Jesus the Savior. Given this background, it becomes evident that when the centurion praises God, his praise must be more than an acknowledgement of Jesus' political innocence. The reader, after all, knows that Jesus is innocent. Rather, in some way it must fit into the wider scheme of God's salvific activity in Jesus.[5]

What the leaders, the soldiers, and the first criminal couldn't grasp was understood by the other criminal and this centurion:

in Jesus the way to salvation is opened up. What the repentant criminal declared is what the centurion recognized. First, the centurion *saw*. Then, when "all the crowds who had gathered there for this spectacle" *saw* what had taken place, "they returned home beating their breasts" (Lk 23:48).

The only other place where Luke writes about people beating their breasts is in 18:13 in reference to the tax collector who recognized his own sinfulness in the presence of the one whom he acknowledged as having a higher power than his. In Luke, to see is to recognize. But this recognition implies admission that people *see* their sins.

Once they had *seen*, their conversion could begin. They could return home; there they could go further into their conversion by taking small steps toward self-surrender. Maybe, just maybe, because they too had seen, their surrender could now begin, and they could experience the embrace that comes with faith—which comes in surrender of self to another's hands.

For those who heard these words of Jesus surrendering his spirit, their own surrender began when they began to beat their breasts. So maybe, just maybe, it must be so with us. Possibly we will be able to say: "Father, into your hands, I commend my Spirit," only after we repent—of our sins or our righteousness—by beating our breasts.

Before we entrust our very spirit into the hands of our God, we must use our hands in repentance to beat our breasts. It's the only way we can go home.

Like the crowds in Luke's gospel, then, for us too the surrender and seeing might end in the embrace of faith.

The older I get, the more events invite me to surrender many things—my ideas and assumptions, my feelings and emotions, my preconceptions and prejudices, my behaviors and expectations of other people and institutions—if I am to be one

whose spirit can be commended to God. This surrender must come before I embrace anything. And this surrender can be multifaceted.

For instance, as I was riding the "tube" in London in 1992, a poster displayed at various subway stations captured my eye. Pictured on the poster was a beach scene inhabited by "bikers," who seemed to be attending "Bike Week" at a place like Daytona Beach where cars and bikes are allowed on the beach. There were bikers in the background and in the foreground, and two women in black bathing suits sitting on chaise longues. Above the rear fender of one of the bikes was a big U.S. flag. In the sky above a plane flew carrying a trailer sign: "Miss Harley Davidson Autograph Party: 9-11."

Between the Harleys in the background and foreground, a balding white man in cut-offs walks on the sand barefooted. He carries a cross one and a half times larger than himself. He's got another cross on his white tee-shirt with some message on it, undecipherable.

I assumed that the man carrying the cross thinks the ones who need to convert and surrender their ways are the bikers. As he walks among them, does he do so in a "righteous" way? I wonder if he ever identifies with those he probably considers sinners. Maybe he is there to be a witness for Christianity to these bikers. But he isn't interacting with any of them, nor they with him. Perhaps he believes he is being a witness to the faith that's in him just by being there.

At the top of the poster was a red sign declaring the name of the show featuring this picture and others. This Carl De Keyzer exhibit, "God, Inc.: The Role of Religion in American Life," would be at The Photographers' Gallery in London.

Originally I thought this was a perfect picture to depict our culture and the traditional symbols of Christianity inviting us to a change of heart. But I found myself beginning to see differently, beyond the crucifying stereotypes of dogmas and compulsion. I found I had to surrender these. I found myself in need of beating my breast. As I contemplated the picture I began to recognize my need to go beyond my attitudes and the experiences that helped shaped my initial response and interpretation. Confronted by my own preconceptions and prejudices, I needed to beat my breast and surrender them in order truly to respond to my Jerusalem and my Temple and all the people they represent—some of whom happened to be pictured on that poster.

Bikers, like many other groups, tend to be a cross section of our culture. For instance, one biker I know controls the largest bank among four or five in his Midwestern city. Other bikers are priests. And, like most groups, there are those with less "laudable" occupations as well. The more I contemplated that picture, the more I realized I had to surrender many ideas about the people riding bikes and about the man carrying the cross as well. Maybe the cross-carrier in that poster is a biker too. Or what if one of those bikers happens to be "Brother Bert"?

I recently was given a postcard-size picture of Brother Bert. From his external appearance, complete with beard and leather, Bert looks just like the stereotypical biker—enough to put the fear of the Lord into your bones. But Bert's shirt proclaims Jesus, and even his bike sports a "Get Saved" sticker. Jesus is Bert's co-rider. On the back of the postcard it says: "I must go until he comes, give until I drop, preach until all know, and work until he stops me. And when he comes for his own, he will have no problem recognizing me. My colors will be quite clear."

Brother Bert has helped me surrender some of my previous images of bikers and instead wonder who among the bikers and cross-carriers are the ones who have truly surrendered to Christ. The resulting embrace has made life more interesting and sur-

prising for me. In the process I have found myself moving from former ways of thinking, learning, and philosophizing.

The beginning of philosophizing as we know it today in the West began with Greek metaphysics. This effort to get to the essence of things gradually became subordinate to the demands of Christian doctrine. But then came René Descartes. With him philosophy ceased being the "handmaid of theology" and the search for universal and objective truth began. The Age of Enlightenment also believed in some underlying rational essence at the core of all things. But then came Immanuel Kant, who questioned the relationship between the knower and the known, between our search and truth itself. Where before the concentration was on the "known," the object, now the "knower," the subject, became of prime importance.

What remained constant from the Greeks on is that the valued knowing belonged to anyone with power over what was known, and this "knowing" reveals domination over the known by the knower — the "privileged position" of the knower. Yet, because it is grounded in domination, it can survive only through oppression of others, who become objects. Again, it implies a kind of scapegoating.

A consequence of this phenomenon has been well expressed by Eleanor M. Godway: "One of the features of privilege apparent in many situations of oppression is that it tends to become invisible to the holders of that privilege, especially if they form a group."[6]

I am gradually coming to realize the wisdom of Eleanor Godway's conclusion: "We have to 'unlearn' what we have been colluding with as we have been coopted by privilege, and the outcome of this unlearning will allow us to handle the violence [of the previous way of thinking and knowing] differently — that is why I make so bold as to refer to [this new way of knowing as] an 'epistemology of the Cross.' "[7]

Epistemology involves a way of knowing or learning. Certainly Jesus' words from the cross, especially "into your hands I commend my spirit," teach us much about the cross's epistemology.

In Surrender and Catch *Kurt Wolff outlines sociologically this "epistemology of the Cross."*[8] *First it involves "surrender." Then comes the "catch." I prefer to use two terms—surrender and embrace—as I look at the way Jesus surrendered in his passion and, in the process, embraced resurrection.*

One of the key elements in the surrender dimension of this way of the cross involves what Wolff calls the "suspension of received notions." Certainly the "received notions" for those around the cross—the leaders, the soldiers, and the thief—was that Jesus should come down from it. But Jesus' words of surrender suspended the conventional wisdom and traditional ways of knowing. This "suspension of received notions" has implications for us as well—even in the way we judge cross-carriers and bikers!

Every authentic spirituality speaks of surrender. Christian spiritualities of surrender find their source in the kenosis *of Jesus and the epistemology of his cross.*

> *Though he was in the form of God,*
> *[he] did not regard equality with God*
> *as something to be exploited,*
> *but* emptied himself *(Phil 2:6).*

To enter this "kenotic" way of surrender, early Christians sought martyrdom. Later its expression took many forms; we find the Jesuits stressing indifference, the Josephites self-emptying, the Franciscans Lady Poverty, and the Carmelites nothing/ness. The seventeenth-century French school counselled abandonment while we in the twentieth century speak of detachment. Buddhists teach the need to enter into nirvana, while people in recovery talk about relinquishment: "letting go and letting God." Ecologists urge simplification.

All of these images suggest other words for surrender. Even as children its concept was at the heart of one of our earliest prayers:

> Now I lay me down to sleep.
> I pray the Lord my soul to keep.
> If I should die before I wake,
> I pray my Lord my soul to take.[9]

Unfortunately, most spiritualities seem to stop at surrender, at becoming detached from our attachments. They stress the cross, the "letting go" or even the "letting God" without talking about the embrace. While surrender represents letting go of the need to control (and even of our need for scapegoats), embrace is paradoxically the result of letting go, the experience of something new never anticipated. It flows from authentic surrender.

I believe that one of the most powerful examples of someone surrendering and experiencing this embrace is Francis's way of relating to lepers.

From Francis's own words, he makes it clear that, following the cultural pattern of his time, he had "received notions" about lepers. "It seemed very bitter to me to see lepers," he wrote in his "Testament."[10] As a youth he would look at their houses only from a distance of two miles, and he would hold his nostrils with his hands.[11] Society's scapegoats were his as well. His "Testament" continues, "The Lord Himself led me among them and I had mercy upon them." This was the surrender. What came with this surrender and his embrace of the leper was the expe-

rience of himself caught in embrace: "And when I left them that which seemed bitter to me was changed into sweetness of soul and body."[12]

Once enveloped in this embrace, he experienced nondiscriminating love. To be with lepers became the continual dei for him. It would be translated in conversion, a new way of thinking, feeling, and acting.

With this surrender and embrace, Francis not only surrendered his spirit into the hands of his heavenly parent; he entered into the lives of his earthly brothers and sisters in the embrace of solidarity. Now God could be embraced as all in all. Francis learned the epistemology of the cross. Such is the consequence (as well as the process) of being able to say: "Into your hands I commend my spirit."

Once we surrender old ways—including, for me, "received notions" about cross-carriers and bikers—and embrace a new vision, we can never be the same.

Woman, Here Is Your Son
... Here Is Your Mother

Meanwhile, standing near the cross of Jesus were his mother, and his mother's sister, Mary the wife of Clopas, and Mary Magdalene. When Jesus saw his mother and the disciple whom he loved standing beside her, he said to his mother, "Woman, here is your son." Then he said to the disciple, "Here is your mother." And from that hour the disciple took her into his own home.

I remember reading, years ago, of a remarkable incident involving two young men in Chicago—one shot by the other. The 14-year-old slayer was apprehended, put on trial, and convicted. As the parents of the young man who had been shot observed their son's assailant—still alive—something prodded them to look further into his story. Against their better judgment, not to mention conventional wisdom, they started visiting him in jail. Initial fear and curiosity changed to attraction and intrigue; they found themselves fascinated with their only son's assassin.

The more they learned about him, the more they came to understand the forces that contributed to his terrible deed. And like most loving parents, when they really understood these dynamics, there was little to forgive. They wondered at a reality now made fresh to them — that so many children have no home while their son's room in theirs stood empty.

The time came when they asked the young man who'd been serving his time if they could take him into their home; if he would allow them to become his adoptive parents. What had transpired nineteen hundred years ago at Calvary was brought to the fourth level of redaction in Chicago. That is, the mystery of the cross was borne out in human struggle and crisis, struggle and crisis that get relived in the human family in every generation and in every culture. In surrendering their anger at the loss of their son, they embraced his killer and took him into their home. A new relationship was forged.

In 1986 I visited our Capuchin brothers working in Panama. At one of the many market areas in Panama City I was impressed by a mola that depicted the scene from the cross where Jesus created the new relationship between his mother, who was about to see her son die, and the beloved disciple, who would make sure she would not be alone.

Molas are the name for the folk art of Cuna women among whom our Capuchin brothers minister in Panama. One of the most frequently used religious themes for molas is the crucifixion:

> Molas depicting the crucifixion conform closely to a standard motif with Christ on the cross surrounded by symbols of the passion. They are most often made with exceptional skill and care. It would almost seem that unless a woman feels confident that she can make a beautiful mola she will not attempt this subject.[1]

The particular mola I bought was not made by one woman but by a group. Maybe there's a message here for us. Perhaps if we

grow in confidence with one another, if we can entrust our-
selves to one another, we too can create a work of awesome
beauty in the way we become the community of beloved ones.
To me, this is the message of belonging and entrustment rep-
resented in the first words of John's Jesus from the cross.

John's passion narrative, like the rest of his gospel, offers a
portrait of Jesus distinct from the synoptics. John's Jesus is lofty
and exalted like the eagle often associated with this evangelist.
His gospel narrative is rich in nuances; signs characterize his
redaction of stories related to the Sign—the Word of God, who
came to dwell among us.

In John's narrative, signs become a symbol, filtered through
Jesus, of God's continued work in the world. Faith becomes
our response, as disciples, to that symbol. Faith is our share in
the Sign. John's passion narrative continues the fertile symbols
and signs found from the gospel's beginning. Indeed, the cross
is the goal, the summit toward which John's whole gospel leads.
It is in itself a sign of salvation. Like Mark's, John's gospel might
be considered a passion story with a very long introduction.

John's portrayal of Jesus' passion presents someone remark-
ably self-possessed and in control of his destiny. Even as Jesus
goes to Jerusalem and to his final hour, he directs the dynamics.
On the way to Golgotha, for instance, unlike the synoptics,
John's Jesus carried the cross by himself (Jn 19:17).

In the passion account, as well as in John's recollection of
Jesus' last words, Jesus demonstrates his self-possession by going
beyond his conflict with those who sought to control and, in
the end, destroy him. He makes it clear that they would have
no control, no power at all, unless it had been given to them
"from above" (Jn 19:11). John explains how they abused that
power.

Far from being "delivered up," the fourth gospel has Jesus

speak of his passion and death as an elevation; he is "lifted up." Rather than a humiliation, the cross is Jesus' glorification. In short, John's narrative of Jesus entails a homecoming that will find him ascending to God. His life will be taken from him by no one; he himself will lay it down while fully in control of his destiny.

When I was at Berkeley I took a course on John's gospel. My professor, John Boyle, maintained that John's gospel is so unified and integrated that we can take any major theme or even expression and develop a wholly connected Johannine theology around it.

One word full of symbolic significance in John's passion narrative can be found in his notion of the "hour." At Cana we observe the first of the signs performed by Jesus and, for the first time, are told about the *hour*. When his mother told Jesus: " 'They have no wine,' . . . Jesus said to her, 'Woman, what concern is that to you and to me? My hour has not yet come' " (Jn 2:3-4). But the hour that had not yet come came in that same hour when Jesus performed "the first of his signs, in Cana of Galilee and revealed his glory; and his disciples believed in him" (Jn 2:11).

As the hours of his life continue, we read about more signs. They all serve as preludes to the real and terribly imminent hour of his passion and death. Knowing "that his hour had come to depart from this world" (Jn 13:1) marks John's introduction of the passion narrative.

An hour denotes a period when "the time has come," a "set time," the period for an appointment. But all these hours, while secularly grounded, are divinely appointed. John's "hour," Gerhard Delling reminds us, includes the notion of Jesus' "obedience to God's direction within the given situation."[2]

Anyone who is serious about John's story of Jesus has connected the scene of Mary at the cross with the first of Jesus' signs at Cana. As we examine this Cana-become-Calvary scene, however, there are some issues that John does not make clear.

The first asks exactly who was there—at the Place of the

Skull, which in Hebrew is called Golgotha—besides the two others crucified with him, "one on either side, with Jesus between them" (Jn 19:17-18).

Unlike the synoptics, who keep Jesus' supporters at a distance, John writes: "Standing *near* the cross of Jesus were his mother, and his mother's sister, Mary the wife of Clopas, and Mary Magdalene" (Jn 19:25). This sounds as though four women stood there. But there could have been three, if we read it: "Standing near the cross of Jesus were his mother; and his mother's sister, Mary the wife of Clopas; and Mary Magdalene." No one really knows whether Jesus' mother's sister was Mary the wife of Clopas or not. There were many Marys in those days—even within the same family—so there could be three instead of four near the cross of Jesus at that hour.

However many women there were at the cross that day, and who they were, a deeper question revolves around John's other statement: "Jesus saw his mother *and the disciple whom he loved* standing beside her . . . " Why didn't this disciple get included earlier in the grouping? And who was this "disciple whom Jesus loved?" Could he have been a *she*?[3]

In John's gospel the term *beloved disciple* is used only five or six times—and only after the Last Supper. There "one of his disciples—the one whom Jesus loved—was reclining next to" Jesus (Jn 13:23). This is the first use of the term. The second time takes place at the cross with this account of Jesus' words to his mother and the beloved one. The third occurs "on the first day of the week," when Mary Magdalene returned from the tomb telling "Simon Peter and the other disciple, the one whom Jesus loved," of the news (Jn 20:2). This disciple "who reached the tomb first" is recorded as the first who "saw and believed" (Jn 20:8). The fourth time we encounter the beloved disciple occurs in the boat when that disciple speaks to Peter regarding the one on the shore who asked them about their catch: "It is the Lord!" (Jn 21:7). Finally, when Peter heard about how his death would glorify God he "turned and saw the disciple whom Jesus loved following them; he was the one who had reclined next to Jesus at the supper" (Jn 21:20). (We might consider a sixth use of the term the conclusion: "This is the disciple who is testifying to these things and has written them, and we know that his testimony is true" (Jn 21:24).

So how do we discover the identity of this mysterious beloved disciple? When I was a serious seminary student studying the scriptures, the tradition was that the beloved disciple was the apostle John. Raymond Brown taught this then, but now Brown has changed his mind and agrees with those who say the beloved disciple was not one of the twelve, though Brown maintains he was an apostle. Some still say he was the evangelist (who today is more often called the redactor or final composer). They insist that the "beloved" one had to have been an eyewitness, and this eyewitness had to have been the redactor.[4] But then others say he was not the redactor, but rather the one who inspired the final writing of what we now know as the gospel according to John.[5]

Over time, many historical figures of the first century have been suggested as the beloved disciple. Some insist it was Peter's secretary, John Mark. He was also, they say, the author of the gospel. Others argue that it was the one who owned the house where Jesus celebrated his Last Supper, because it would be natural for a host to sit at his right. It may have been a priest, others proffer, because the "beloved" hesitated to enter the tomb; a priest could not risk ritual contamination. Still others say it was a priest because the beloved disciple was known by the High Priest and had access to the Sanhedrin. Others think he was a former disciple of John the Baptist or a blood brother of Jesus who became the last to join the twelve but was the first in discipleship. Still others argue it was a Judean disciple called Lazarus, of Martha and Mary fame; he was the only male mentioned in the scriptures as loved by Jesus. One writer connects Qumran's "Teacher of Righteousness" with the beloved one.

Others surmise that the beloved disciple was more than a historical person, that is, he was an *idealization* of a historical

person, "the epitome of believer, disciple, beloved, and witness."[6] Some, such as Donald Senior and Raymond Brown see
the beloved disciple as a representative or a symbolic figure,[7]
someone the author uses to serve as a paradigm of authentic
discipleship. "While a real person," Raymond Brown notes,
"the Beloved Disciple functions in the gospel as the embodi-
ment of Johannine idealism: All Christians are disciples and
among them greatness is determined by a loving relationship
to Jesus, not by function or office."

In this vein, Rudolph Bultmann thought that the Beloved
One was a representative of Gentile Christianity (while Peter
represented Jewish Christianity). Alv Kragerud says he symbolized Christian prophetism. Byrne and Culpepper believe he was
the founder and head of the Johannine school during its creation. Others argue this historical person has paradigmatic
meaning. But all of them have concluded that the Beloved
Disciple had to have been historical. As Raymond Brown writes,
"The thesis that he is purely fictional or only an ideal figure is
quite implausible. It would mean that the author of John 21:20-
30 was deceived or deceptive, for he reports the distress in the
community over the Beloved Disciple's death."[8]

There are still others, however, who disagree. Precisely
because the person was not named, they conclude the beloved
disciple may never have been historical but was a figure of the
redactor used for a specific literary purpose.

Whatever, since John presents the beloved disciple as the
first who did not see but in that lack of vision "saw and
believed" (Jn 20:8), I believe — as someone who has not seen —
that the beloved disciple is the paradigm of what discipleship
must mean for us. I find support for my position in Jesus' words
to Peter after the resurrection. Peter asked Jesus what would
happen to the beloved disciple. Jesus replied: " 'If it is my will
that he remain until I come, what is that to you? Follow me!'
So the rumor spread in the community that this disciple would
not die. Yet Jesus did not say to him that he would not die,

but, 'If it is my will that he remain until I come, what is that to you?' " (Jn 21:22-23).

Perhaps this was the redactor's way of grappling with the probable fact that the beloved disciple had died at the time of the writing of John's gospel. I believe, though, that the stress should be placed not on his possible death, but on the beloved disciple's life as paradigmatic for all of us who strive to be disciples in the church. Then every one of us — past, present, and future — is to "remain until I come." We will be with the Risen Lord when we live by the faith that believes even if it doesn't see.

We believers — who are trying to live at the fourth level of redaction, who are trying to make the scriptures come alive for us — are to be the beloved disciples. We can better understand what really happened then, and must happen now, as we read John's recollection of the first words of Jesus from the cross: "When Jesus saw his mother and the disciple whom he loved standing beside her, he said to his mother, 'Woman, here is your son.' Then he said to the disciple, 'Here is your mother.' And from that hour the disciple took her into his home" (Jn 19:26-27).

In the Mediterranean world of the first century, kinship constituted the core of all human relationships. Maintaining and strengthening family bonds and the honor of the clan, especially the home, was imperative. From his prologue until this pericope at the cross John shows Jesus establishing a new kinship grouping among his disciples. In the prologue of his gospel John says that Jesus, the Word-become-human, "came to his own home" (*eis ta ídia*). Now, at the cross, the image of homecoming is repeated when John writes that the beloved disciple "took her into his home" (*eis ta ídia*). As I. de la Potterie shows, *eis ta ídia* does not mean "home" in the sense that Mary moved in with John, but rather that they created a new relationship, one which made them responsible for each other.[9]

When, at the beginning of his gospel, John describes the way Jesus created a community of disciples, he recalled Jesus saying:

"Come and see" (Jn 1:39; see 1:46). When they did, John says, they "remained with him" (Jn 1:39). So, remaining with Jesus constitutes discipleship. Remaining in his love defines us as beloved disciples. Remaining until he comes is the promise of the Spirit for faithful disciples. So, because we believe, we remain with Mary. We take her home so she can remain with us, challenging and inspiring us by her faith to become the community of disciples of her Son.

We call this community *church*. This church is the new family of Jesus constituted in his blood with Mary and the beloved disciple (read: us) as its family members. As Mark Stibbe writes, "In giving these two people to one another, Jesus begins a new family at the moment of his death."[10]

I really should not be using the word *Mary* for the one who is never called that name. Indeed Mary is not mentioned by that name in any part of John. Instead, she is called "woman" and "mother," both at Cana and at the cross. And, because both terms imply household relations, their meanings further substantiate the structure of John's house-church, the community of disciples his gospel tries to construct.

Building on the work of M. Girard, Joseph A. Grassi makes a strong argument for restructuring the seven signs constituting John's gospel in a way that revolves around Cana and the cross at the beginning and end, with the story of the loaves in the middle:

(1) the wedding feast at Cana (2:1-12)
(2) the restoration of the dying son (4:46-54)
(3) the Sabbath healing at Bethesda (5:1-16)
(4) the multiplication of loaves (6:1-71)
(5) the Sabbath healing of the blind man (9:1-41)
(6) the restoration of Lazarus to life (11:1-44)
(7) the great hour of Jesus: his mother, the cross, and the issue of blood and water from Jesus' side (19:25-37).[11]

From the beginning of John's gospel (where his family ties are recalled, with his mother, the "woman,") and in the middle (where the loaves are multiplied), until the end (where Jesus reconstitutes his family as beloved disciples with his mother), the church is composed of those who remain with each other, who take each other into their own home.

At the cross Jesus puts the beloved disciple into his place in his natural family. In the beloved disciple, who is representative of those who have not seen but still believe, Jesus forms a new family of faith. Just as Mary was key in executing the first sign that led to the disciples' believing, she is at the heart of the final sign, when disciples who do not see signs still believe.

"Mary's part and witness in these signs," Grassi concludes, "are a key to her role as mother, as well as a key to understanding the beloved disciple as a legitimate successor to Jesus and a model for both believer and community."[12]

But if the beloved disciple is a model for believer and community, how do we recognize the role of mother that this woman we call Mary engendered for believers and community? I used to think Jesus was almost cold in not calling this woman Mother, or even Mary. But "*woman!*" I even tried to defend Jesus, saying he *really* wasn't talking down to her, as it seemed; I said *woman* was a term of respect used in that part of the world at that time. But no women were respected at that time (see Jn 4:27); they didn't count (see Matt 14:21; 15:38). It was the proper thing for sons to talk that way to their mothers; so, while Jesus might not have been respectful in our sense of the word, at that time he was being quite proper.

The word John uses for "woman" is *gunē*; *gunē* refers to a wife in familial relationships, in a household, to the one who helps create a home. So, in saying to his mother, "Woman, here is your son," and to the disciple whom he loved, "Here is your mother," John is talking about the new home that we help build up when we enter the community of disciples and take Mary, who typifies what makes a household of faith, into our home. Earlier, at Cana, when Jesus' hour had not yet come, the "woman" had to have faith. But now, at the cross, when

Jesus' hour had come, the one he called "woman" now became mother to those who have faith.

William S. Kurz has written that the readers of John's gospel are to identify with the beloved disciple as similarly beloved disciples "to whom Jesus entrusts his secrets, his church, and the task of loving each other and witnessing to him 'until he comes' (John 21:22-23)."[13] I'd add to Kurz's insight that, precisely because we are the beloved disciples, what Jesus truly has entrusted to us is his mother, the "woman" who now exists to help us become the community of believers.

So, in John's gospel, if it was in the beginning when the first sign was performed, the sign that showed that his "hour" had truly come, and it was in the middle when the sign came in the breaking of the bread, which began to separate the believers from those who looked for signs, and at the end when his "hour" brought him to the cross, then, where Mary is, the beloved disciple must be. Where the church of the beloved disciples is, there is Mary. And where Mary is, there must be the community of beloved disciples. And the beloved disciples are those who believe.

Moving to a deeper level of redaction—to our own lives—if each of us is to be the beloved disciple, then we realize that the commission that came from that cross *before* the disciple took her to his home represents the start of the creation of a new house, which today we call church. While this church is inseparable from Mary, we cannot give Mary, in this church, any greater role in this endeavor than we give ourselves. We must take care today, when some seem more concerned about Mary's role in the church than about their call to be beloved disciples, so that the church can become—and remain—the church. It all depends on faith.

Before we really embrace the Johannine vision of Mary and its power for us in the church, I believe we need to surrender many

of our symbolic interpretations of her. Despite what John says about Mary, our magazines and newspapers continually relate new stories about the mother of Jesus connected to an appearance here, an appearance there, appearances everywhere, it seems.

While I was writing these reflections during Lent of 1993 I visited a parish in Southern California where "Special Edition II" of Our Lady Queen of Peace was available in the vestibule. One of its articles, which details scores of alleged apparitions, is entitled, "Why has Mary come?" It states:

> *Everywhere you turn, new reports of miraculous manifestations of God and of the Blessed Virgin are being reported. In America alone, in just the past twelve months, new reports of apparitions, weeping statues and pictures with messages from Jesus and His Mother, Mary, have come in from almost every state. San Antonio, TX; Lake Ridge, VA; Barberton, OH; Marlboro, NJ; Conyers, GA; Arlington, VA; Grosse Pointe Woods, MI; Bella Vista, AK; Ellsworth, OH; Isabela, PR; Middletown, OH; Garden Grove, CA; Prescott Valley, AZ; El Ranchito, TX; Chicago, IL; Fountain Valley, CA; Watsonville, CA; Lakeworth, FL; Seattle, WA; Trenton, NJ; Tickfaw, LA; St. John, WI; Lorena, TX; St. Louis, MO; Denver, CO; Cold Spring, KY; Scottsdale, AZ; Santa Maria, CA; Cleveland, OH; Ontario, Canada; Green Bay, WI; Buffalo, NY; Wantagh, NY; Uniontown, PA; Sacramento, CA; Duluth, MN; Thornton, CA; Dunmore, PA; Hillside, IL; East Stroudsburg, PA are just a few of the latest reports. Elsewhere, new reports are coming in from Ireland, the Ukraine, Africa, the Middle East, Philippines, Yugoslavia, Italy, Brazil, Chile, Guatemala, Malta, Australia and Czechoslovakia: to name a few. Why has Mary come?[14]*

Not long after U.S. News & World Report had a cover feature about alleged tears coming from a statue of Mary in Virginia:

"The Case of the Weeping Madonna." It explained: "Statues of the Virgin Mary are shedding tears. Or so claims a young Virginia priest. Is it a miracle or a hoax?"[15] *A year before I had picked up a Good Friday column in* USA Today *by Barbara Reynolds, one of its regular columnists, entitled: "Why Does a Statue of the Virgin Mary Weep?" Reflecting on a visit she made to the suburban church in Lake Ridge, Virginia, she too asked, "Why does she weep?" She wondered:*

> *Is she weeping for all the mothers who must also watch their sons being crucified on the street corners of America? Does she weep because the Catholic church fails to ordain those of her sex to the priesthood while calling sexism "evil"? Does she weep because the powerful don't weep; don't aid the powerless? Are we at the point where wooden statues must cry out because some human hearts have turned to stone?*[16]

One of the reasons why "some human hearts have turned to stone" may be the way religion, including Mary's role, has been commercialized. When the rosary is advertised along with non-dairy creamer and cereal, and when one alleged apparition after another is cast in doubt, it is little wonder that some hearts become cynical, if not stony.

Whenever I hear about the latest apparition of Mary, which yet again emphasizes people's concern with what she allegedly says or means, I return to John's gospel to listen to the last words he records coming from her lips. For me, these serve as her testament—and God's word to me as well. To be a beloved disciple, I must "do whatever he tells you" (Jn 2:5). And what he tells me, as he entrusts his mother to me as a beloved disciple, is that the future of our church will fulfill his vision when we who have had Mary entrusted to our care begin to entrust ourselves not only to her, but to each other. Then we will have created a home we can call church.

The first hour began when, in the midst of his family and friends, Mary recognized a need and ushered the way for Jesus to perform the first of his signs. Now, as we hear these words of Jesus from the cross, the new hour begins when we perform the last of his signs and become the community of disciples that we have been called to be.

~ 6 ~

I Am Thirsty

When Jesus knew that all was now finished, he said (in order to fulfill the scripture), "I am thirsty." A jar full of sour wine was standing there. So they put a sponge full of the wine on a branch of hyssop and held it to his mouth.

Recently I was with a woman dying of cancer. Although I've not been with all that many people as they were dying, I've noticed two things. First is the manner in which they breathe, and second is how dry, even parched, their tongues can become. So too with this woman. She couldn't communicate in any way. Perhaps she was not even conscious. Still, my heart went out to her, and I tried to touch her tongue with some water. It would not revive her, certainly, but at least it might refresh. It seemed like I was touching leather, raw unfinished leather.

As Jesus was dying, his thirst too must have made his tongue like leather, only adding to the pain of crucifixion. The Journal of the American Medical Association once carried an article where doctors speculated about the symptoms Jesus must have suffered as he hung on the cross. They noted that Jesus suffered great emotional stress, as evidenced by hematidrosis (sweating blood), undoubtedly intensified by his disciples' abandoning him and the humiliating physical beating. The brutal scourging

*would have caused intense pain and appreciable blood loss.
These probably contributed to a state of preshock trauma. The
most likely causes of death by crucifixion were hypovolemic
shock and exhaustion asphyxia. Other possible contributing fac-
tors included dehydration, stress-induced arrhythmias, and con-
gestive heart failure with a rapid accumulation of fluids.*[1]

*Anyone who was crucified would at least lose a great amount
of body fluid and thus would experience dehydration. Even from
a purely human viewpoint (which is never simply the way John
presents his story of Jesus) it is not surprising that from his cross
Jesus would say, "I am thirsty."*

Recall how John's narrative interprets the passion, with Jesus
very much in control of its evolution. Here again Jesus directs
the dynamics. As John tells us, Jesus "knew that all was now
finished." And so, "to fulfill the scripture," he said, "I am
thirsty."

In all the other accounts of Jesus' last words that fulfill the
scriptures, we can find the exact quotation. For instance, when
Mark and Matthew recall Jesus saying, "My God, my God, why
have you forsaken me?" (Matt 27:46; Mk 15:34), we find it
word for word in the first line of Psalm 22. Likewise, in Luke's
account, Jesus' final prayer to his Father repeats the prayer of
the psalmist in Psalm 31: "Into your hand I commit my spirit."
Besides integrating these words of the Hebrew scriptures with
the last words of Jesus, other narrative sections in the passion
have no fewer than thirteen and possibly as many as seventeen
psalm texts appearing as quotations or allusions. Thus it is puz-
zling to discover that there is no scripture that says "I am
thirsty." It stands as an exception, an utterance without a firm
precedent, a reported psalm verse without a psalm.

The majority of commentators point to Psalm 69 as a possible source: "They gave me poison for food, and for my thirst they gave me vinegar to drink" (v. 12), but I think this is stretching. G. Bampfylde notes: "This is not entirely satisfactory for although this scripture refers to thirst, it does not use the words 'I thirst.' Also, since John consistently quotes the scriptures fulfilled in the events of the Lord's passion, one would expect him to have quoted Ps. lxix 21 after he recorded that Jesus had been given vinegar to drink."[2]

Other commentators point to the passage in Psalm 22, the key psalm used in the passion narratives. It describes the suffering just one who trusts in God: "My mouth is dried up like a potsherd, and my tongue sticks to my jaws; you lay me in the dust of death" (v. 15). But this passage, while alluding to thirst, does not use the word itself, nor does the suffering one ask for a drink.

So, when Jesus said, at the point of his death, that he was thirsty, *in fulfillment of the scriptures*, there must be something more involved than these words about thirst. That "something more" can be understood through further examination of John's redaction.

Jesus' life here is at the point of its completion. So we must consider his *whole life*, which has fulfilled the scriptures. This is the work God has given him to do; it is now fulfilled. So Jesus simply says he is thirsty; it is as direct and honest as that.

At their meals soldiers of that arid land drank a potent wine (*óxlos*). Some translations call it "strong," others "sour," and others "sharp." *Óxlos* relieved thirst more effectively than water and was cheaper than regular wine. People of moderate means, like soldiers, would carry at least one jar full of that kind of wine.

It was common in that part of the Mediterranean for people to give drink to someone thirsty, understanding that such an action would be pleasing to God. What is surprising at Golgotha is that they shared it with the one they had crucified. These god-fearing folk who saw that a "jar full of sour wine was standing there . . . put a sponge full of the wine on a branch of hyssop and held it to his mouth" (Jn 19:29). It isn't clear exactly who offered Jesus the wine, sour though it may have been. "They" could have included his mother or his other relatives or the beloved disciple. Most likely, if we rely on the synoptics, it was the soldiers who shared their drink with him.

What appears clear, however—though contrary to popular opinion and populist piety—is that their action, at least here in John, seems prompted by mercy. Only Luke's version makes the motivation of those who gave Jesus the sour wine possibly hostile, part mockery (Lk 23:36).

So if the point isn't that Jesus said "I am thirsty" to fulfill the scriptures, and if the drink offered him was drunk by all commoners like himself, what does John intend when he says, "After this, Jesus, knowing that all was now finished, said, to fulfill the scripture, 'I am thirsty' "? What exactly was being fulfilled here?

In all other places where John speaks of some scripture being fulfilled, he uses the word *pleróō*. However, to describe the "fulfillment" taking place here he uses the word *teleióō*. And when John uses *teleióō* elsewhere in his gospel, it involves something Jesus does that "completes" the work of the One who sent him into the world (Jn 4:34; 5:36; 17:4). In explaining how John uses *teleióō*, G. Bampfylde states: "The Son has been given a particular assignment by His Father, and He does everything in order to bring this to its fulfillment. *Teléō* indicates the final action that brings the assignment to its fulfillment. When His ministry on earth ceases or, in other words, when His hour has come, this is the point at which the 'perfection' of 'the work' is achieved, and the results of its consummation can *begin*."[3]

How the results of this consummation begin can be understood more clearly, I believe, if we probe further the notion of Jesus saying: "I am thirsty" in John's gospel.

The first place where Jesus speaks of thirst in John's gospel comes in the encounter he had in the Samaritan city called Sychar with a Samaritan woman at Jacob's well. Jesus asked for a drink (Jn 4:47). John records Jesus saying: " 'Everyone who drinks of this water will be thirsty again, but those who drink of the water that I will give them will never be thirsty. The water that I will give will become in them a spring of water gushing up to eternal life.' The woman said to him, 'Sir, give me this water, so that I may never be thirsty or have to keep coming here to draw water' " (Jn 4:13-15).

While the woman was away testifying in the town of her encounter with Jesus, John's Jesus enters into an extended passage progressing from water to food, and from completing his work to the very labor into which the disciples were entering: "My food is to do the will of him who sent me and to complete his work. . . . I sent you to reap that for which you did not labor. Others have labored, and you have entered into their labor" (Jn 4:34, 38). John makes it clear that, in this first instance where Jesus speaks of others' thirst, and in this last instance when he speaks of his own thirst, the "hour" was about noon.

The coming of his hour on the cross, when he completed the work he was given to do, now becomes the hour when the disciples, the beloved disciples, are to continue the work he gave them to do: the work of being his new family with the woman he called mother. When Jesus received the wine, he said, "It is finished." But what had finished was merely *his* work. The work of his beloved disciples—with his Mother in their company—had to continue. To enable this work to continue he "gave up his spirit" (Jn 19:30). Then "one of the soldiers pierced his side with a spear, and at once blood and *water* came out" (Jn 19:34).

Earlier John connected believing and coming to Jesus, with drinking in order to alleviate thirst: "Let anyone who is thirsty come to me, and let the one who believes in me drink." Now, John adds, after speaking of the blood and water coming from the side of Jesus, "He had said this about the Spirit, which believers in him were to receive; for as yet there was no Spirit, because Jesus was not yet glorified" (Jn 7:37-39). In John, Jesus' glorification comes within the event of his crucifixion when Jesus, always in full control of the dynamics at work, "gave up" (*paradidónai*) his spirit. But to whom did Jesus "give up" his spirit, since *paradidónai* means to hand something over *to another*?

The synoptics use the word *paradidónai* to refer to others who delivered up Jesus to the cross, but John uses it only once in that sense, referring to the sin of the one who "handed him over" (Jn 19:11). However, here John uses the word *paradidónai* to refer to the way Jesus, in charge of his own destiny, handed over his spirit. But again we can ask, *to whom is this spirit given?*

Donald Senior writes: "The phrase 'hand over his spirit' in 19:30 refers to the moment of death itself and the focus is on Jesus' return to God. While a double-meaning cannot be excluded for such a phrase, it is more likely that the evangelist does not intend to describe at this point the donation of the Spirit."[4] I find John's gospel, however, full of double-meanings and discern here a multifaceted meaning developed only as we read on.

Upon giving over his spirit, John continues, "one of the soldiers pierced his side with a spear, and at once blood and water came out" (Jn 19:34). The reason John records this, he states, is to provide testimony, so that "you" — each one of us — "also may believe" (Jn 19:35). Somehow John is connecting Jesus' death with the readers, the beloved disciples whose belief makes them the ones called to continue the work of Jesus. This can be done only in the Spirit, by sharing in the water and the blood from the side of Jesus.

Raymond E. Brown posits that, while Matthew and Luke also describe Jesus' death as a yielding up of his life spirit,

> John seems to play upon the idea that Jesus handed over the (Holy) Spirit to those at the foot of the cross, in particular to his mother, who symbolizes the Church, the new people of God, and to the Beloved Disciple who sym-

bolizes the Christian. In vii 39 John affirmed that those who believed in Jesus were to receive the Spirit once Jesus had been glorified, and so it would not be inappropriate that at this climactic moment in the hour of glorification there would be a symbolic reference to the giving of the Spirit.[5]

The testimony regarding Jesus giving up his spirit, and the blood and water coming from his side may be John's, but John's testimony authenticates a deeper witness. He writes elsewhere: "This is the one who came by water and blood, Jesus Christ, not with the water only but with the water and the blood. And the Spirit is the one that testifies, for the Spirit is the truth. There are three that testify: the Spirit and the water and the blood, and these three agree" (1 Jn 5:6-8).

Now the Spirit, the water, and the blood are handed over to those who believe. The beloved disciples with Mary "his mother" are to continue the work originally entrusted to them by Jesus. In this way Jesus "gave up" his spirit. G. Bampfylde notes that the word should be taken to mean "transmission to one's successor." Those who succeed Jesus are "those faithful few standing by the cross [who] will receive the benefits of the Son's accomplished work. They are to be His inheritors, but particularly so is this true of the beloved disciple." Bampfylde concludes, "This helps us further to establish that he [John] was thinking of Jesus' transmission of the Holy Spirit to successors, the most important successor for the needs of the readers and the authority of this gospel being the beloved disciple."[6]

So now we come to understand that the only way the scriptures will be fulfilled will be when we who thirst find in the living waters of Jesus, and in the blood from his side, the gift of his Spirit enabling us to complete the work of God entrusted originally to him. But this will never happen in our lives unless we thirst. And it will never happen for those of us who thirst unless we come to him and drink of his living waters. When we begin to drink of these living waters, we take on the work he's entrusted to us. Just as his life was the fulfillment of the scriptures, those scriptures then might begin to be fulfilled in us.

Recently a young man, Andy Kastenholtz, a youth minister in a white suburban Milwaukee parish, shared with me a dilemma that was causing him no little anxiety.

"You know, Mike," he said to me with tears in his eyes, "the more I read of Jesus in the gospels, and the more I read of what's occurring in the institutional church, the more I conclude that I can no longer find Jesus in the Catholic church."

For Andy Kastenholtz the norms of Jesus found in the gospels no longer constitute the ways of thinking, self-reflection, and behavior found in institutional Roman Catholicism.

What is a young man like Andy Kastenholtz to do in such a dilemma?

Francis of Assisi also was a young man. He had visions of grandeur, which he based on the ways of thinking, and imagination, and behavior of the dominant — and dominating — culture of his time, the Holy Roman Empire. It was at odds with the papacy and its power.

The result was that Francis took on the patterns of his culture. His first biographer notes that imitating its "habits for a long time, he became even more vain and proud."[7] In such a culture these ways had become the ways of people "who are considered Christian in name," yet they show "in themselves nothing of the Christian religion either in their daily lives or in their conduct, [and] they take refuge under the mere name of Christianity.''

In the next paragraph his biographer Celano indicates the surrender that then began in Francis: ''The hand of the Lord therefore came upon him and a change was wrought by the right hand of the Most High; that through him an assurance might be granted to sinners that they had been restored to grace and that he might become an example to all of conversion to God.''[8]

After narrating how this process of surrender found Francis abandoning the militarism and consumerism, the elitism and phobias of his time, Celano tells how Francis embraced the gospel as the norm and basis for his life. In a church-controlled culture he no longer found ''fulfilling,'' he embraced Christ as the constitutive and normative dimension of his life. What Jesus had fulfilled on the cross now could continue in Francis himself.

Soon after this Francis surrendered his society's ways and embraced the leper, but he still did not know how his life should be directed in order to live out the gospel in his culture and in his church.

One day Francis happened to be near the little church of San Damiano. It represented what had happened, I think, to the church of his times—it was in ruins, abandoned by so many. However, Francis went in and in words that indicate the continual surrender taking place in him, Celano writes that ''he found himself other than he had been when he entered. While he was thus affected, something unheard of before happened to him: the painted image of Christ crucified moved its lips and spoke. Calling him by name it said: 'Francis, go, repair my house, which, as you see, is falling completely to ruin.' ''[9]

That painted image, if you examine it, has Mary and John (the apostle and evangelist) on the left side, along with a little man

in the corner, who was the one whom the artist depicted as giving Jesus the sour wine. On the right side is Mary's sister and Salome, along with the man who probably commissioned the icon, with the heads of many behind him.

We've seen that John most likely wasn't the beloved disciple, so I interpret those many "heads" on the San Damiano cross to refer to the "many" members of the community. As the new beloved disciple, we each must find ourself on the cross if the scriptures are to be fulfilled in us.

What happened then to Francis is my dream for us. Celano notes: "From then on compassion for the crucified was rooted in his holy soul, and, as it can be piously supposed, the stigmata of the venerable passion were deeply imprinted in his heart, though not as yet upon his flesh."[10]

Celano details how Francis went about in that militaristic and consumeristic culture and in that chauvinistic and clerical church trying to make the gospel the core of his life and the norm for his living. But in the community of beloved disciples, which he founded to continue his dream, he offered a gospel way of living as a norm, that the brotherhood might constitute its very life. And his partner Clare did the same with her sisterhood. In their rules for their followers, both wrote that the form of their lives together should be to observe the gospel.

So, not only in their own lives, but in their own communities within the decaying religion, they were to give birth to a revitalized church by a new kind of surrender and embrace that would be called the brotherhood and sisterhood. Their vision of communities of beloved brothers and sisters, living the gospel, would be the creation and maintenance of what I have called "communities of entrustment."[11] Francis articulated such a community, which would reflect the kind of community envisioned by John's Jesus when he entrusted his mother and the beloved disciple to each other:

> And wherever the brothers may be together or meet [other] brothers, let them give witness that they are members of one family. And let each one confidently make known his need to the other, for, if a mother has such care and love for her son born according to the flesh (cf. 1 Thes 2:7), should not someone love and care for his brother according to the Spirit even more diligently?[12]

When brothers and sisters can confidently make their needs known to each other, they create the context for the kind of community where entrustment can create bonds of commitment.

Celano shows what happened to Francis, who found it "extremely necessary that the Gospel calling be fulfilled in him who was to be the minister of the Gospel in faith and in truth."[13] In a passage that has become my favorite, detailing what happened as a result of his obsession with "living the gospel," Celano has already detailed the stigmata that Francis received, marking him with the wounds of Christ Crucified. Now, as Francis experienced great pain, physical from his bodily suffering and emotional from watching his dream decay in front of his cauterized eyes,

> his companion once said: "Father, you have always sought refuge in the Scriptures, and they have always given you remedies for your pains. I pray you to have something read to you from the prophets; perhaps your spirit will rejoice in the Lord." The saint said to him: "It is good to read the testimonies of the Scripture; it is good to seek the Lord our God in them. As for me, however, I have already made so much of Scripture my own that I have more than enough to meditate on and revolve in my mind.

I need no more, son; I know Christ, the poor crucified one.''[14]

In time, just as the vision of church expressed in Jesus' proclamation of the reign of God took on the patterns of the culture until it was falling into ruin, the same degeneration of "preserving" the Franciscan institution took over instead of the gospel that was to be its norm and constitution. What happened is best summarized in the words of the imaginary Pope Kiril in Morris L. West's Shoes of the Fisherman:

> "[A] man like St. Francis of Assisi, for instance. What does he really mean? A complete break with the pattern of history. . . . A man born out of due time. A sudden, unexplained revival of the primitive spirit of Christianity. The work he began still continues. . . . But it is not the same. The revolution is over. The revolutionaries have become conformists. The little brothers of the Little Poor Man are rattling alms boxes in the railway square or dealing in real estate to the profit of the order." He laughed quietly. "Of course, that isn't the whole story. They teach, they preach, they do the work of God as best they know, but it is no longer a revolution.''[15]

Today too, our ways of thinking, and imagining, and being the community of beloved disciples, the church, have taken on the ways of our culture. Perhaps we find it harder to hear Jesus from the cross saying, "I thirst," when those words are drowned out by ubiquitous slogans for soft drinks and beer.

On the one hand, we can believe the ads and rely on this world's beverages to satisfy our thirst. On the other, we can hear the words from the cross that indicate the fulfillment of the scriptures in our hearts is what will satisfy our thirst. When the gospel message starts getting fulfilled in us, we too should be able to say: "Let whoever is thirsty come to me." Because we have been given the Spirit, the hungry and thirsty, the alone and the lonely, the abusers and abused, the perpetrators and the victims, the dominating and oppressed (all of whom are in us) should be able to come to us and entrust themselves to us. Then they too might experience what it means to be beloved disciples in a community wherein all can confidently make known their needs. And when we come to this place, if we've been to the cross, all will be nourished by a well that never runs dry.

It Is Finished

When Jesus knew that all was now finished, he said (in order to fulfill the scripture), "I am thirsty." A jar full of sour wine was standing there. So they put a sponge full of the wine on a branch of hyssop and held it to his mouth. When Jesus had received the wine, he said, "It is finished." Then he bowed his head and gave up his spirit.

During the time I was drafting this book I happened one day to be on a flight from California back home. Seated next to me was a white man with long hair, slightly overweight. He wore a white denim cowboy shirt, black denim pants, white cowboy boots with black trim, and silver accessories. From the way the flight attendants deferred to him I knew I was in the company of a well-known person but I couldn't figure out who he might be. From his attire I surmised he might be a country singer.

Finally, my curiosity got the best of me. I asked him who he was. "Jeff Fennholt," he responded. That didn't help me either. When I pleaded my ignorance again, he explained that he had had the lead role of Jesus in the original Broadway cast of Jesus Christ Superstar.

"How providential," I thought. I wondered what he thought as he said those seven last words—not just once on a cross cen-

turies ago but in my generation every day except Mondays for two and a half years!

When I asked him, he told me that at the time of the show, he was not a believer. In fact, the night the play opened, which was the week that his picture as Jesus Christ Superstar was featured on the cover of Time, he came "that close," he said (as he showed me his thumb and finger a half inch apart) to "killing myself." His wife had to drag him from their terrace to keep him from hurling himself to the street below.

As he had gone through rehearsals and prepared for the open-ing, he had been high on drugs and dope and alcohol and sex. He was playing at the role of Jesus. It had not been fulfilled in him; he had not entered the role at all. Now, it had caught up with him. "I wasn't just hearing the words," he said, recalling what happened in the play as he hung on the cross. "I was hearing voices all the time. God was speaking. Jesus was speak-ing. The demons were speaking. And then I'd go at it with four women at one time in the dressing room. But I kept hearing those voices and one of those voices kept saying to me: 'Why have you forsaken me?' "

Finally, after two and a half years of drugs, drinking, and wom-anizing, combined with his acting, the voices became louder. He left the show. He weighed a mere 125 pounds, and his stomach was hemorrhaging.

When I asked him what influenced him to change his life, he told me of some "Christians" who had come to his house to lay new carpet. "I had gotten so screwed up with drugs and stuff, and I was getting fear and panic attacks continually, that when these men said they wanted to pray for me, I went to my room."

There he struggled with questioning whether these "Christians" were of God or of the occult, which he had been involved in as well.

"After a couple of hours wrestling with this dilemma," he said, "I finally felt a need to pray, but I didn't know how to pray or to whom to pray. So I said: 'Whoever you are. I'm so confused. And I'm falling apart. I can't continue living this way with this fear and these panic attacks and these voices. I'm going to go down those stairs and ask them to pray for me. If they are light, let me listen. If they kill me because they are in the occult, know I died trying to find you.' "

So Jeff went down to where the Christians were laying the carpet. "I'm not interested in Jesus," he told them. "But I'm looking for God and what God wants of me." "But Jesus is God," they said.

Then Jeff heard himself saying something like: "Jesus, if you are the Lord, I need your help." In admitting his need for help Jeff made his surrender. His experience of embrace would come almost immediately.

As the carpet-layers prayed over him, he experienced Christ in a way he could never have imagined. "I felt like an anvil was taken from my back. My mind became clear for the first time in years. The fear and panic attacks were lifted out. This weight was lifted from me and my mind became clear."

That day he asked Jesus to come into his life. "I've never been the same since," he said simply, honestly, and thankfully.

Now Jeff Fennholt performs in concerts and as host on "Highway to Heaven," a television show, singing Christian rock music.

When I finally told Jeff that I was writing a book on the seven last words of Jesus, his reaction was spontaneous: "Those are the seven most powerful words I have ever spoken. But do you know which ones are the most important, the most incredible?" And when I asked him what he thought, he said, without hesitation, "It is finished."

He went on to explain, "Jesus could have said, 'I've had it; I'm freaking out; I'm out of here; I'm not going to take this anymore.' But instead he said, 'It is finished.' If he hadn't said those words, all those other words from the cross would have been in vain. But he stayed there until he finished what he had to do."

What Jeff said next told me that he realized that what Jesus had finished meant a beginning for Jeff Fennholt: "If he hadn't said, 'It is finished,' I would have died on drugs and been in hell. I would have been finished instead of him."

The work given Jesus was finished on the cross. But now, at the fourth level, where the scriptures get fulfilled in us, Jeff Fennholt realized his work was just beginning. He was on his way to the Midwest to testify to what God had begun in him.

Given what was discussed in the previous chapter, which connected Jesus' words "I am thirsty" with the fulfillment of the scriptures, there's not much more that can be said here because, for John, the final fulfillment (*teleióō*) of Jesus' work was realized when Jesus said, "It is finished." The very word he used to say "It is finished" is a word implying fulfillment: *tetélestai.*

Donald Senior notes that this final word spoken by Jesus represents "a word in perfect harmony with the tone of the entire Johannine Passion story: 'It is finished (*tetélestai*)' (19:3). The very same word, used twice before in this scene (see 19:28), brings the life of Jesus to its goal. He has 'completed' his work and returned to God."[1]

The *Revised Standard Version* of John's gospel, which is closest to the original Greek, translates Jesus' final words "It is finished." However, a closer examination of the text reveals it to be more exact if we were to read: "It is fulfilled." If we used the Greek, the final scene at the point of Jesus' death would read:

> After this, when Jesus knew that all was now *tetélestai*, he said (in order to *teleothai* the scripture), "I am thirsty," A jar full of sour wine was standing there. So they put a sponge full of the wine on a branch of hyssop and held it to his mouth. When Jesus had received the wine, he said, "*Tetélestai*." Then he bowed his head and gave up his spirit.

In his article on the word *tetelestai* in the *Theological Dictionary of the New Testament*, Gerhard Delling writes that "the word from the cross in Jn. 19:30 is explained by v. 28: Everything that God commissioned Jesus to do has been 'completed,' the saving work whose earthly completion according to Jn. is at the cross."[2]

The word John chooses to describe the end for Jesus referred not only to his passion and his death, which fulfilled his messianic mission, but to the hour toward which *all* of Jesus' works were directed from the beginning. In Jesus view, all the words and works of his life could end, for they would be continued in the community of beloved disciples, the community of faith founded from his side.

J. Terrence Forestell notes, however:

> The remarkable thing about the Johannine presentation is the fact that the evangelist considers the death of Jesus

rather than his resurrection as the completion of his work. This point is even emphasized by the repetition of *tetélestai* and the unique choice of *teleiōthē* in place of the more common *plerōthē* [for words meaning "to fulfill"]. The death of Jesus on the cross is the completion of his work because it is his passage from this world to the Father. And at the same time it is a passage that is accomplished out of love for those [who live] in obedience to the Father's will.[3]

Earlier, during the evening of his life, Jesus had declared that he had completed the work God had given him to do (Jn 17:4). But this work was not fulfilled until that crucifixion for which he was sanctifying himself. "When it is," A. R. C. Leaney notes: "and he gives up his life he says that it is completed (19:30)." Leaney, however, adds, "In one respect this sanctification is for the sake of his followers (1QH 6:6-9; Jn 17:19). In the case of Jesus, it is said that 'I sanctify myself, that they may be sanctified in the truth.' "[4]

Jesus had accomplished what he had come to do. For him it was finished; now it would be the responsibility of his followers, sanctified in truth, to keep his word, to continue his work. Then "my Father will love them, and we will come to them and make our home with them" (Jn 14:23).

In the beginning, God had begun a work (*ergon*) and finished it (Gn 2:2 [2x], 3). Then, to continue the work itself, God's word became flesh in Jesus, and when that Word made its home among us (Jn 1:14), Jesus' works, as far as Jesus' life was concerned, were done to finish what God had begun (Jn 4:34; 5:36; 6:28; 9:4; 10:25, 32, 37, 38; 14:10, 11; 15:24; 17:4). The work begun by God in the very beginning was brought to completion in Jesus; that is what *he* finished. But that which he finished is not yet done. Others must continue the work if it is to be finished in the end. Now it is up to the beloved disciples—who are called to remain until all the work of God and Jesus is fulfilled—to believe and act on that belief in such a way that the work will continue (see Jn 10:38; 14:11).

We who are to be the community of the beloved ones, can be comforted by the parting words Jesus spoke the night before he embraced the cross: "*Amen, Amen* I tell you, the one who believes in me will also do the works that I do and, in fact, will do greater works than these, because I am going to the Father. I will do whatever you ask in my name, so that the Father may be glorified in the Son. If in my name you ask me for anything, I will do it" (Jn 14:12-14).

And until God, through us, concludes that work begun in the beginning, until it is truly accomplished, the hour will not have come. Until that time, we, as the beloved disciples, have our work cut out for us if the scriptures are to be fulfilled in us and our work.

John narrated the words "it is finished," because his community needed to hear them so its members would fulfill them in their lives, in their words, in their deeds. Most commentators are clear that John's gospel was written to a community in conflict and crisis. Synagogue life was structured, with status, roles, duties, and expectations that defined people's place. The expulsion of the followers of Jesus left them without any structure to speak of. The consequence was traumatic; they were a tooth separated from its roots.

Furthermore, the larger Roman environment and its attendant cultural imperatives created more conflict and crisis. Because many Christians refused to take part in the civil life of the empire and in the cults used to reinforce its domination, Christians were mightily despised.

Unwilling to run from the conflict, the community of beloved disciples struggled to continue the vision of its founder. John's gospel was written to provide them hope. According to Adela Yarbro Collins: "The gospel responds to this crisis in two ways. On the one hand, it expresses a vision of community life which could compensate for the isolation from other social groups. On the other hand, it provides a view of reality which reinforces the integrity of this community over against a hostile world."[5]

Our own contemporary communities, called church, will maintain evangelical integrity, it seems to me, to the degree that we find—as in John's original community—ourselves in conflict with our synagogues and churches, with our culture and our empire. Every crisis involves a challenge or a turning point that confronts us to move from the present. If we find nothing about which we are in crisis, we will have no work to finish. But if we find nothing about which we are in crisis, we will have been "finished" as well.

That the work still needs to be done and that the crucifixion of Christ continues in our world today in its conflicts and crises became very clear to me when I received the portrait "Christ in the Favela." It was sketched for me by my Brazilian Capuchin confrere, Celso Beaudignon (see page 110).

When I visited Rio Grande de Sol in southern Brazil in 1986, Celso took me to visit friends and coworkers who lived in a huge favella where he had worked as a student seminarian.

I remember one family in particular whose squatter house was squeaky clean. The father had a regular job; he was a bus driver. They longed for housing elsewhere, but because they didn't have connections in the system, and because they were from the wrong part of the city, they would probably be nailed to this cross of tin and wood they called home until they died. But they considered themselves lucky. Their shanty was not next to the freeways, where they would breathe the fumes of unregulated car exhausts, or in one of the gulleys, where it could

be washed away by the waters of the floods that came and went so frequently.

So, Celso's picture continually reminds me, it is not finished yet — for us.

This realization was driven home to me with great force in 1992 as I celebrated Good Friday at my parish church, St. Benedict's in Milwaukee. St. Ben's traditionally celebrates its Good Friday service not only within the church building but also in the world which surrounds us. This year it took place at MacArthur Square, bordered by the police station, and the jail, and the courthouse. The theme of our Good Friday liturgy was stated quite clearly: "In solidarity with victims of violence."

We gathered in the church. As we entered we received a spent cartridge from some gun along with a cross made from the "caution" tape used at scenes of violence and tragedy. On each cross was the picture of a victim, someone murdered on the streets of Milwaukee in 1991. On my "caution cross" was the 150th victim of violence: Michael Tourme, a Milwaukee police sergeant shot while chasing a burglary suspect, November 18, 1991.

After initial reflections and prayers, the passion of Jesus according to John was proclaimed. Then, following a large cross, we processed to MacArthur Square. There seven individuals reflected on seven manifestations of the violence which permeates our culture and our church: in our jails and our justice system; in our racism and in drugs; in our families and toward our youth; and, finally, the violence endured by the physically and mentally ill. In response to each reflection and prayer we sang the Taize refrain:

> *O Lord, hear my prayer;*
> *O Lord, hear my prayer.*

> *When I call, answer me.*
> *O Lord, hear my prayer;*
> *O Lord, hear my prayer.*
> *Come and listen to me.*

Of all the reflections, the one that spoke most deeply to me that day came from Reverend Antone Jenkins, a black man who serves as a chaplain in the jail across the street and who graces our living room on Fridays with his searing reflections on the scriptures:

> *"Finished, it's finished, nearly finished, it must be nearly finished. It is finished! I can't be punished anymore." So echo the words of the suffering Christ from the cross intertwined with the opening lines from Beckett's play, Endgame. But for the men, women, and children who find themselves outside the mainstream of American society: the downtrodden — the downcast, and the downhearted — of their suffering there appears to be no end. No, it's not finished. . . .*

> *We have been summoned here at this most sacred hour by the eternal Spirit because collectively we realize we cannot afford any longer to be spectators of the suffering of our neighbor. . . . We are called as witnesses so that we may raise our collective voices to let America know that it's not finished. . . .*

> *No, it's not finished until there is justice in the courtroom and people are judged not on the color of their skin but on the merits of the evidence. No, it's not finished until African American males are not four times as likely to be arrested as their white counterparts. No, it's not finished until there are no more Rodney Kings being beaten by white policemen. No, it's not finished as long as African American males are subjected to longer and stiffer prison*

sentences than their white counterparts. No, it's not finished until African American, Indian, and Hispanic males
are no longer more likely to be convicted than white
males. No, it's not finished until justice in America is not
based on one's ability to pay for a skilled attorney. No,
America, it's not finished until every able-bodied person
who wants to work is guaranteed employment at a living
wage. No, no, it's not finished until every person in this
country is off the streets and given decent housing. No,
it's not finished until every crack house becomes a safe
house, until children cease to be neglected, until the eld-
erly don't have to eat dog food to survive, until racism
becomes an obsolete word in our vocabulary, until the
church ceases to be the most segregated place in America
on Sunday. No, it's not finished.[6]

Reverend Antone Jenkins limited his remarks that day to the
work that still needs to be done in America.

But the work is not finished in Rio Grande de Sol, or anywhere
else people hunger and thirst, anywhere people seek living
waters to satisfy them. When Jesus received the wine from
whomever it was who cared enough to quench his thirst, he
said, "It is finished." Then he, but not we, "bowed his head
and gave up his spirit" (Jn 19:30).

We know we cannot yet bow our heads because there are too
many bowed heads around us that need to be lifted up in the
Spirit. And, as far as our discipleship is concerned, until we
complete our work, it will never be finished.

Notes

Introduction

1. Vernon K. Robbins, "The Crucifixion and the Speech of Jesus," *Forum* 4 (1988), 33-46.

2. I have tried to be faithful in my exegetical approach to the "interactive hermeneutic" I outlined in my *House of Disciples: Church, Economics, and Justice in Matthew* (Maryknoll, N.Y.: Orbis Books, 1988), 5-17. Again, in this book, as in *House*, I see the fusion of the gospels' first-century "horizon" and our own today as revolving around basic relations among persons and resources. Because of the more popular style of this book, I would ask readers wanting a more critical development of my hermeneutic to examine *House*.

3. See Sandra Schneiders, *The Revelatory Text: Interpreting the New Testament as Sacred Scripture* (San Francisco: Harper, 1991), 1, 99. Also Edward Schillebeeckx, *Church: The Human Story of God* (New York: Crossroad, 1990), especially 11-42.

4. Schneiders, 2. Schneiders offers a very clear and lucid interpretation of the hermeneutics or meaning that invites us to move from the first three levels to the fourth.

5. "Eight Groups in Milwaukee Target of FBI Probe," *Milwaukee Sentinel*, January 28, 1988, 2.

6. Xavier John Seubert, OFM, "Contemporary Art and the Expanded Death of the Human Jesus," *New Theology Review* 6 (1993), 36.

1. Why Have You Forsaken Me?

1. Paul Likoudis, "After Retreat, Buffalo Priests Complain of a New Form of Clerical Sex Abuse," *The Wanderer* 126, February 4, 1993, 6.
2. Joachim Jeremias, *The Lord's Prayer*, trans. John Reumann (Philadelphia: Fortress, 1964), 19-20.
3. Gerard Rosse, *The Cry of Jesus on the Cross: A Biblical and Theological Study*, trans. Stephen Wentworth Arndt (New York/Mahwah: Paulist, 1987), 64.
4. Johannes Schneider, "*Oneidízō*," in *Theological Dictionary of the New Testament* 5, ed. Gerhard Friedrich, trans. Geoffrey Bromiley (Grand Rapids: Eerdmans, 1967), 240.
5. Donald Senior, C.P., *The Passion of Jesus in the Gospel of Mark* (Wilmington: Michael Glazier, 1984), 123.
6. Ethelbert Stauffer, "*Boáō*," in *Theological Dictionary of the New Testament* 1, ed. Gerhard Kittel, trans. Geoffrey W. Bromiley (Grand Rapids: Eerdmans, 1964), 627.
7. Daryl D. Schmidt, *The Gospel of Mark* (Sonoma, Calif.: Polebridge, 1990), 4.
8. Howard Clark Kee, *Community of the New Age: Studies in Mark's Gospel* (Philadelphia: Westminster Press, 1977), 176ff; Ched Myers, *Binding the Strong Man: A Political Reading of Mark's Story of Jesus* (Maryknoll, N.Y.: Orbis Books, 1987), 41.
9. John R. Donahue, *Are You the Christ?* (Missoula, Mont.: Society of Biblical Literature, 1973), 222-23.
10. Myers, *Binding the Strong Man*, 384.
11. Obituary, " 'Rock-and-Roll' Comedian Sam Kinison Killed in Car Accident," *The Washington Post*, April 12, 1992, B11.
12. Richard N. Ostling, "The Church Search," *Time*, April 5, 1993, 45.
13. Ad in *The Wall Street Journal*, April 12, 1988.

2. Father, Forgive Them

1. Stephen J. Abler and Wade Lambert, "Common Criminals: Just about Everyone Violates Some Laws, Even Model Citizens," *The Wall Street Journal*, March 12, 1993.

2. Frank J. Matera, "The Death of Jesus According to Luke: A Question of Sources," *The Catholic Biblical Quarterly* 47 (1985), 476.

3. Marcus J. Borg, "The Jesus Seminar and the Passion Sayings," *Forum* 3 (1987), 87. Only 8 percent of the Fellows agreed that Jesus undoubtedly said these words or something very similar.

4. Gottfried Quell and Gottlob Schrenk, "*Pater*," in *Theological Dictionary of the New Testament* 5, ed. Gerhard Friedrich (Grand Rapids: Eerdmans, 1967), 985.

5. J. Massyngbaerde Ford, "Reconciliation and Forgiveness in Luke's Gospel," in *Political Issues in Luke-Acts*, ed. Richard J. Cassidy and Philip J. Scharper (Maryknoll, New York: Orbis Books, 1983), 96.

6. Raymond Brown, S.S., *New Testament Essays* (New York/Ramsey: Paulist Press, 1965), 248.

7. René Girard, *The Scapegoat*, trans. Yvonne Freccero (Baltimore: Johns Hopkins University Press, 1986), 111.

8. Bruce J. Malina and Jerome H. Neyrey, "Conflict in Luke-Acts: Labelling and Deviance Theory," in *The Social World of Luke-Acts: Models for Interpretation*, ed. Jerome H. Neyrey (Peabody, Mass.: Hendrickson, 1991), 117.

9. Girard, *The Scapegoat*, 37, 38.

10. Johanna Neuman, "U.S. Report Details Serbian Atrocities," *USA Today*, October 23, 1992.

11. Lance Morrow, "I Spoke . . . as a Brother: A Pardon from the Pontiff, a Lesson in Forgiveness for a Troubled World," *Time*, January 9, 1984, 33.

3. Today You Will Be with Me in Paradise

1. Dan Parks, "Cleric Says Dahmer Could Go to Heaven," *The Milwaukee Sentinel*, February 5, 1992, 1.

2. Bruce J. Malina and Jerome H. Neyrey, "Conflict in Luke-Acts: Labelling and Deviance Theory," in *The Social World of Luke-Acts: Models for Interpretation*, ed. Jerome H. Neyrey (Peabody, Mass.: Hendrickson, 1991), 98.

3. Joseph Fitzmyer, *The Gospel According to Luke,* Anchor Bible (Garden City, N.Y.: Doubleday, 1981-85), 1501.

4. Donald Senior, *The Passion of Jesus in the Gospel of Luke* (Wilmington: Michael Glazier, 1989), 26.

5. Richard J. Dillon, "The Psalms of the Suffering Just in the Accounts of Jesus' Passion," *Worship* 61 (1987), 434.

6. For more on this see Otto Michel, "*Mimnēskomai,*" in *Theological Dictionary of the New Testament* 4, ed. Gerhard Kittel, trans. Geoffrey W. Bromiley (Grand Rapids: Eerdmans, 1973), 676.

7. Joachim Jeremias, "*Parádeisos,*" in *Theological Dictionary of the New Testament* 5, ed. Gerhard Friedrich, trans. Geoffrey W. Bromiley (Grand Rapids: Eerdmans, 1973), 770-71.

4. Into Your Hands I Commend My Spirit

1. There is dispute on what the rending of the Temple curtain means in Luke. One school sees it as a sign of the Temple's destruction; another of the abrogation of the Temple cult; and another of the opening of a way for humanity to God's presence. See Sylva, "The Temple Curtain and Jesus' Death in the Gospel of Luke," *Journal of Biblical Literature* 105 (1986), 241, n. 7.

2. Walter Grundmann, "*Dei,*" in *Theological Dictionary of the New Testament* 2, ed. Gerhard Kittel, trans. Geoffrey W. Bromiley (Grand Rapids: Eerdmans, 1982), 22. See also Matera, "The Death of Jesus According to Luke: A Question of Sources," 476ff; Senior, *The Passion of Jesus in the Gospel of Luke*, 35-39.

3. Donald Senior, C.P., *The Passion of Jesus in the Gospel of Luke* (Wilmington: Michael Glazier, 1989), 168.

4. Jerome Neyrey, S.J., *The Passion according to Luke: A Redaction Study of Luke's Soteriology* (New York/Mahwah: Paulist Press, 1985), 147.

5. Matera, "The Death of Jesus According to Luke: A Question of Sources," 480-81.

6. Eleanor M. Godway, "Faith *and* Knowledge in Crisis: Towards an Epistemology of the Cross," *Listening* 27 (1992), 102.

I am thankful to Ms. Godway for her reflections which have helped shape my thoughts in this section.

7. Ibid., 103.

8. Kurt H. Wolff, *Surrender and Catch: Experience and Interpretation Today* (Boston: D. Reidel, 1976).

9. I am indebted to Virginia Pratt, one of the retreatants at Mercy Center, for making the connection with traditional spiritualities of detachment and this child's prayer.

10. Francis of Assisi, "Testament," 1, in Regis J. Armstrong and Ignatius C. Brady, trans., *Francis and Clare: The Complete Works* (New York: Paulist, 1982), 154.

11. Thomas of Celano, *First Life of Saint Francis* 17, in Marion A. Habig, *St. Francis of Assisi: Writings and Early Biographies* (Chicago: Franciscan Herald, 1973), 243.

12. Ibid.

5. Woman, Here Is Your Son

1. Ann Parker and Avon Neal, *Molas: Folk Art of the Cuna Indians* (Barre, Mass.: Barre Publishing, 1977), 137.

2. Gerhard Delling, "Ōra," in *Theological Dictionary of the New Testament* 9, ed. Gerhard Kittel, trans. Geoffrey W. Bromiley (Grand Rapids: Eerdmans, 1974), 678.

3. Sandra M. Schneiders notes that "there are enough ambiguities in the fourth gospel's few clues to the identity of the evangelist and/or the Beloved Disciple to at least raise a serious question about whether one or both might have been a woman." See Sandra M. Schneiders, *The Revelatory Text: Interpreting the New Testament as Sacred Scripture* (San Francisco: Harper, 1991), 185.

4. This view is based on a reading of John 21: 20 and 24. See, for example, Charles John Ellicott and Donald Guthrie.

5. For example, see the works of F. M. Braun, A. M. Hunter, Rudolf Schnackenburg.

6. R. Collins, "The Representative Figures in the Fourth Gospel," *Downside Review* 94 (1976), 130; John F. O'Grady, "The Role of the Beloved Disciple," *Biblical Theology Bulletin* 9 (1979), 58.

7. This seems to be the position of Donald Senior, C.P., *The Passion Narrative in the Gospel of John* (Wilmington: Michael Glazier, 1991), 110-14.

8. Raymond E. Brown, *The Community of the Beloved Disciple: The Life, Loves, and Hates of an Individual Church in New Testament Times* (New York: Paulist Press, 1979), 31.

9. I. de la Potterie, "La parole de Jésus 'Voici ta Mère' el l'accueil du Disciple (Jn 19,27b)," *Marianum* 36 (1974), 1-39.

10. Mark W. Stibbe, *John as Storyteller: Narrative Criticism and the Fourth Gospel* (Cambridge: Cambridge University Press, 1992), 151.

11. Joseph A. Grassi, "The Role of Jesus' Mother in John's Gospel: A Reappraisal," *The Catholic Biblical Quarterly* 48 (1986), 69.

12. Ibid., 80.

13. William S. Kurz, "The Beloved Disciple and Implied Readers," *Biblical Theology Bulletin* 19 (1984), 100.

14. "Special Report: Why Has Mary Come?," *Our Lady Queen of Peace*, Special Edition II (Winter 1993).

15. *U.S. News & World Report* (March 29, 1993).

16. Barbara Reynolds, "Why Does a Statue of the Virgin Mary Weep?," *USA Today* (April 17, 1992), 15A.

6. I Am Thirsty

1. William D. Edwards, M.D., Wesley J. Gabel, M.Div., and Floyd E. Hosmer, M.S., AMI, "On the Physical Death of Jesus Christ," *Journal of the American Medical Association* 255 (1986), 1455-63.

2. G. Bampfylde, "John xix 28: A Case for a Different Translation," *Novum Testamentum* 11 (1969), 251.

3. Ibid., 256.

4. Donald Senior, C.P., *The Passion of Jesus in the Gospel of John* (Collegeville, Minn.: The Liturgical Press, 1991), 119.

5. Raymond E. Brown, S.S., *The Gospel According to John* (Garden City, N.Y.: Doubleday, 1970), 931.

6. Bampfylde, "John xix 28," 256.

7. Thomas of Celano, *First Life of St. Francis*, 1, in *St. Francis of Assisi: Writings and Early Biographies*, ed. Marion A. Habig (Chicago: Franciscan Herald Press, 1973), 229-30.

8. Ibid., 2, 231.

9. Ibid., 370.

10. Ibid., 10, 371.

11. Michael H. Crosby, OFMCap, "Trust and Distrust and the Future of Community," *Human Development* 15 (1994).

12. Francis of Assisi (VI, 7-8), in Armstrong and Brady, *Francis and Clare: The Complete Works* (New York/Mahwah: Paulist Press), 141. The words are repeated in Clare's Rule as well (VIII, 9, p. 220).

13. Thomas of Celano, *First Life of St. Francis*, 7, 235.

14. Thomas of Celano, *Second Life of St. Francis*, 105, in Habig, *St. Francis of Assisi: Writings and Early Biographies*, 448.

15. Morris L. West, *The Shoes of the Fisherman* (New York: William Morrow, 1963), 270.

7. It Is Finished

1. Donald Senior, C.P., *The Passion of Jesus in the Gospel of John* (Collegeville, Minn.: The Liturgical Press, 1991), 118.

2. Gerhard Delling, "*Télos*," in *Theological Dictionary of the New Testament*, 8, ed. Gerhard Friedrich, trans. Geoffrey W. Bromiley (Grand Rapids: Eerdmans, 1979), 59.

3. J. Terence Forestell, *The Word of the Cross* (Rome: Biblical Institute, 1974), 88.

4. A.R.C. Leaney, "The Johannine Paraclete and the Dead Sea Scrolls," in *John and the Dead Sea Scrolls*, ed. James H. Charlesworth (New York: Crossroad, 1991), 51.

5. Adela Yarbro Collins, "Crisis and Community in John's Gospel," *Theology Digest* 27 (1979), 317. Much the same interpretation can be found in Bruce J. Malina, *The Gospel of John in Socio-linguistic Perspective* (Berkeley, Calif.: Center for Hermeneutical Studies in Hellenistic and Modern Cultures, 1984).

6. Rev. Antone Jenkins, "Finished," Good Friday Reflection at MacArthur Square (1993). Available from the author.

Bibliography

Bampfylde, G. 1969. "John xix 28: A Case for a Different Translation," *Novum Testamentum* 11.

Bauer, Walter. 1952. *A Greek-English Lexicon of the New Testament and Other Early Christian Literature.* Trans. William F. Arndt and F. Wilbur Gingrich. Chicago: The University of Chicago; Cambridge: University Press.

Bishop, Jim. 1957. *The Day Christ Died.* New York: Harper.

Borg, Marcus. 1987. "The Jesus Seminar and the Passion Sayings," *Forum* 3.

Braun, F. M. 1959. *Jean le Theologien et san evangile dans l'eglise ancienne.* Paris: J. Gabalda.

Brown, Raymond, S.S. 1984. *The Churches the Apostles Left Behind.* New York/Ramsey: Paulist Press.

————. 1979. *The Community of the Beloved Disciple: The Life, Loves, and Hates of an Individual Church in New Testament Times.* New York: Paulist Press.

————. 1970. *The Gospel According to John.* Garden City, N.Y.: Doubleday.

————. 1965. *New Testament Essays.* New York/Ramsey: Paulist Press.

————, et al. 1978. *Mary in the New Testament.* Philadelphia: Fortress Press.

Bultmann, Rudolf. 1971. *The Gospel of John: A Commentary.* Trans. G. R. Beasley-Murray. Oxford: Blackwell.

Byrne, Brendan. 1992. "Beloved Disciple." In *The Anchor Bible Dictionary* 1, ed. David Noel Freedman. New York: Doubleday.

Clare of Assisi, "The Rule of St. Clare." In *Francis and Clare: The Complete Works.* 1982. Trans. Regis J. Armstrong and Ignatius C. Brady. New York/Mahwah: Paulist Press.

Collins, Adela Yarbro. 1979. "Crisis and Community in John's Gospel." *Theology Digest* 27.

Collins, R. 1976. "The Representative Figures in the Fourth Gospel," *Downside Review* 94.

Conrad, Paul. 1993. Political cartoon. *Los Angeles Times* (March 17).

Crosby, Michael. 1991. *The Dysfunctional Church: Addiction and Codependency in the Family of Catholicism*. Notre Dame, Ind.: Ave Maria Press.

———. 1987. *House of Disciples: Church, Economics, and Justice in Matthew*. Maryknoll, New York: Orbis Books.

———. 1994. "Trust and Distrust and the Future of Community," *Human Development* 15.

Cullman, Oscar. 1976. *The Johannine Circle*. Trans. John Bowden. Philadelphia: Westminster Press.

Culpepper, R. Alan. 1978. "The Passion Narrative in Mark," *Review and Expositor* 75.

———. 1975. *The Johannine School: An Evaluation of the Johannine-School Hypothesis Based on an Investigation of the Nature of Ancient Schools*. Missoula, Mont.: Scholars Press.

Daube, D. 1961. "For They Know Not What They Do," *Texte und Untersuchungen* 79.

Delling, Gerhard. 1974. "Ōra." In Gerhard Kittel. *Theological Dictionary of the New Testament*, 9. Trans. Geoffrey W. Bromiley. Grand Rapids: Eerdmans.

———. 1979. "*Télos*." In Gerhard Friedrich. *Theological Dictionary of the New Testament*, 8. Trans. Geoffrey W. Bromiley. Grand Rapids: Eerdmans.

Dillon, Richard J. 1987. "The Psalms of the Suffering Just in the Accounts of Jesus' Passion," *Worship* 61.

Donahue, John R. 1973. *Are You the Christ?* Missoula, Mont.: Society of Biblical Literature.

Ellicott, Charles John. 1971. *Ellicott's Bible Commentary*. Grand Rapids: Zondervan.

Ellis, E. Earle. 1981. *The Gospel of Luke*. Grand Rapids: Eerdmans.

Fennholt, Jeff. n.d. "Out of Darkness." 155 East C Street, #D-313, Upland, Calif. 91786.

Fitzmyer, Joseph. 1989. *Luke the Theologian: Aspects of His Teaching.* New York/Mahwah: Paulist Press.

————. 1985. *The Gospel According to Luke X-XXIV.* New York. Doubleday.

Ford, J. Massyngbaerde. 1983. "Reconciliation and Forgiveness in Luke's Gospel." In Richard J. Cassidy and Philip J. Scharper. *Political Issues in Luke-Acts.* Maryknoll, New York: Orbis Books.

Forestell, J. Terence, C.S.B. 1974. *The Word of the Cross: Salvation as Revelation in the Fourth Gospel.* Rome: Biblical Insititute.

Francis of Assisi, "Testament," 1 and "The Later Rule" I.1. In *Francis and Clare: The Complete Works.* 1982. Trans. Regis J. Armstrong and Ignatius C. Brady. New York/Mahwah: Paulist Press.

Friedrich, Gerhard. 1981ff. *Theological Dictionary of the New Testament.* Trans. Geoffrey Bromiley. Grand Rapids: Eerdmans. (Volumes 5-9; other volumes edited by Gerhard Kittel.)

Girard, René. 1986. *The Scapegoat.* Trans. Yvonne Freccero. Baltimore: Johns Hopkins University Press.

Godway, Eleanor M. 1992. "Faith and Knowledge in Crisis: Towards and Epistemology of the Cross," *Listening* 27.

Grassi, Joseph A. 1986. "The Role of Jesus' Mother in John's Gospel: A Reappraisal," *The Catholic Biblical Quarterly* 48.

Guthrie, Donald. 1979. "John." In D. Guthrie. *The New Bible Commentary,* rev. Grand Rapids: Eerdmans.

Hunter, A. M. 1965. *The Gospel According to John.* Cambridge: The University Press.

Jeremias, Joachim. 1964. *The Lord's Prayer.* Trans. John Reumann. Philadelphia: Fortress.

Kee, Howard Clark. 1977. *Community of the New Age: Studies in Mark's Gospel.* Philadelphia: Westminster Press.

Kittel, Gerhard. 1981ff. *Theological Dictionary of the New Testament.* Trans. Geoffrey Bromiley. Grand Rapids: Eerdmans. (Volumes 1-4; other volumes edited by Gerhard Friedrich.)

Kleinknecht, Hermann, et al. 1982. "*Pneuma.*" In Gerhard Friedrich. *Theological Dictionary of the New Testament* 6.

Kragerud, Alv. 1959. *Der Lieblingsjunger im Johannesevangelium.* Oslo: Univeritatsverlag.

Kurz, William S. 1989. "The Beloved Disciple and Implied Reader." *Journal of Biblical Literature* 19.

Leaney, A.R.C. 1991. "The Johannine Paraclete and the Dead Sea Scrolls." In *John and the Dead Sea Scrolls*. Ed. James H. Charlesworth. New York: Crossroad.

Likoudis, Paul. 1993. "After Retreat, Buffalo Priests Complain of a New Form of Clerical Sex Abuse," *The Wanderer* 126 (February 4).

Lohse, Eduard. 1979. "Cheír." In Gerhard Friedrich. *Theological Dictionary of the New Testament* 9. Trans. Geoffrey W. Bromiley. Grand Rapids: Eerdmans.

Loisy, Alfred. 1950. *The Origins of the New Testament*. New York: Macmillan.

Malina, Bruce J. 1984. *The Gospel of John in Socio-linguistic Perspective: Protocol of the Forty-eighth Colloquy*. Berkeley, Calif.: Center for Hermeneutical Studies in Hellenistic and Modern Culture.

Malina, Bruce J., and Jerome H. Neyrey. 1991. "Conflict in Luke-Acts: Labelling and Deviance Theory." In *The Social World of Luke-Acts: Models for Interpretation*. Ed. Jerome H. Neyrey. Peabody, Mass.: Hendrickson.

Marshall, Howard. 1978. *Commentary on Luke*. Grand Rapids: Eerdmans.

Matera, Frank J. 1985. "The Death of Jesus According to Luke: A Question of Sources." *The Catholic Biblical Quarterly* 47.

McCormick, Patrick, C.M. 1989. *Sin as Addiction*. New York/Mahwah: Paulist Press.

Moore, Sebastian. 1977. *The Crucified Jesus Is No Stranger*. Minneapolis: Seabury.

Myers, Ched. 1987. *Binding the Strong Man: A Political Reading of Mark's Story of Jesus*. Maryknoll, N.Y.: Orbis Books.

Neyrey, Jerome, S.J. 1985. *The Passion according to Luke: A Redaction Study of Luke's Soteriology*. New York/Mahwah: Paulist Press.

Oepke, Albrecht. 1968. "Guné." In Gerhard Kittel, *Theological Dictionary of the New Testament* 1. Grand Rapids: Eerdmans.

O'Grady, John F. 1979. "The Role of the Beloved Disciple," *Biblical Theology Bulletin* 9.

Ostling, Richard N. 1993. "The Church Search," *Time* (April 5).

Parker, Ann, and Avon Neal. 1977. *Molas: Folk Art of the Cuna Indians*. Barre, Mass.: Barre Publishing.

Potterie, de la, I. 1974. "La parole de Jésus 'Voici ta Mére' el l'accueil du Disciple (Jn 19,27b)." *Marianum* 36.

Quell, Gottfried, and Gottlob Schrenk. 1967. "Pater." In Gerhard Friedrich. *Theological Dictionary of the New Testament* 5. Grand Rapids: Eerdmans.

Robbins, Vernon K. 1988. "The Crucifixion and the Speech of Jesus." *Forum* 4: 33-46.

Rosse, Gerard. 1987. *The Cry of Jesus on the Cross: A Biblical and Theological Study*. Trans. Stephen Wentworth Arndt. New York/ Mahwah: Paulist Press.

Schillebeeckx, Edward. 1990. *Church: The Human Story of God*. New York: Crossroad.

Schmidt, Daryl D. 1990. *The Gospel of Mark*. Sonoma, Calif.: Polebridge.

Schnackenburg, Rudolf. 1982. *The Gospel According to Matthew*. New York: Crossroad.

Schneider, Johannes. 1967. "Oneidízō." In Gerhard Friedrich. *Theological Dictionary of the New Testament* 5. Grand Rapids: Eerdmans.

Schneiders, Sandra M. 1991. *The Revelatory Text: Interpreting the New Testament as Sacred Scripture*. San Francisco: Harper.

Senior, Donald, C.P. 1991. *The Passion Narrative in the Gospel of John*. Wilmington: Michael Glazier.

———. 1991. *The Passion of Jesus in the Gospel of Matthew*. Collegeville, Minn.: The Liturgical Press.

———. 1989. *The Passion of Jesus in the Gospel of Luke*. Wilmington: Michael Glazier.

———. 1984. *The Passion of Jesus in the Gospel of Mark*. Wilmington: Michael Glazier.

Seubert, Xavier John, OFM. 1993. "Contemporary Art and the Expanded Death of the Human Jesus." *New Theology Review* 6: 36.

Sheen, Fulton J. 1958. *Life of Christ*. New York: McGraw-Hill.

Stauffer, Ethelbert. 1964. "Boáō." In Gerhard Kittel. *Theological*

128   BIBLIOGRAPHY

Dictionary of the New Testament 1. Grand Rapids: Eerdmans.

Stibbe, Mark W. 1992. *John as Storyteller: Narrative Criticism and the Fourth Gospel*. Cambridge: Cambridge University Press.

Sylva, Dennis D. 1986. "The Temple Curtain and Jesus' Death in the Gospel of Luke," *Journal of Biblical Literature* 105.

Talbert, Charles H. 1982. *Reading Luke: A Literary and Theological Commentary on the Third Gospel*. New York: Crossroad.

Thomas of Celano, *First Life of St. Francis* and *Second Life of St. Francis*. In Marion A. Habig. 1973. *St. Francis of Assisi: Writings and Early Biographies*. Chicago: Franciscan Herald Press.

West, Morris L. 1963. *The Shoes of the Fisherman*. New York: William Morrow.

Wolff, Kurt H. 1976. *Surrender and Catch: Experience and Interpretation Today*. Boston: D. Reidel.

————. 1977. "Toward Understanding the Radicalness of Surrender." *Sociological Analysis* 38.

In addition, I wish to acknowledge the following works, which served to stimulate my thinking about many of the ideas I've developed in this book. I recommend them to the reader wholeheartedly.

Chicago Studies, 1986. Vol. 25, No. 1 (April). Mundelein, Illinois: Civitas Dei Foundation. This entire issue, entitled "Passion, Death and Resurrection of Jesus," is devoted to the Passion narratives.

Krietzer, Larry. 1991. "The Seven Sayings of Jesus from the Cross: Observations on Order and Presentation in the New Testament, Literature, and Cinema," *The New Blackfriars* 72. Krietzer's insights were particularly helpful in shaping my approach to the Introduction.